THE
MEDIA
IN
BLACK
AND
WHITE

THE
MEDIA
IN
BLACK
AND
WHITE

EVERETTE E. DENNIS AND
EDWARD C. PEASE EDITORS

TRANSACTION PUBLISHERS
NEW BRUNSWICK (U.S.A.) AND LONDON (U.K.)

Library of Congress Catalog Number: 96-5598
ISBN: 1-56000-873-3
Printed in the United States of America

Library of Congress Cataloging-in-Publication Data

The media in black and white / edited by Everette E. Dennis and Edward C.
  Pease.
    p. cm.
  Originally published as summer 1994 issue of Media studies journal.
  Includes bibliographical references and index.
  ISBN 1-56000-873-3
  1. Mass media and race relations—United States. 2. United States—
Ethnic relations. I. Dennis, Everette E. II. Pease, Edward C.
P94.5.M55M43   1996
302.23'08—dc20   96-5598
                                                            CIP

Contents

"For reporters, race can be a treacherous subject, raising questions that go to the heart of the journalist's craft," observes the author, a *Newsweek* contributing editor and former Media Studies Center fellow. "Today, though we live in a world that is increasingly multicultural, much of conventional journalism remains fixated on the lives of the white and the wealthy." The result, he says, is tension in the newsroom, the news product and the news consumer.

The 30 years since the zenith of the civil rights movement have brought a "paradox of desegregation," contends the author, chairman of Columbia University's African-American research center and author of numerous books on race in America. Improvements aside, "U.S. race relations in the 1990s have been unambiguously negative," he writes. "Media, film and educational institutions have a decisive role to play in overturning America's pervasive images of inequality."

"Immigrants have always made Americans uneasy," as the associate director of the Center for the New American Community in Washington points out. That uneasiness is growing in the 1990s as new waves of illegal immigrants spill over the borders and are accused of a range of social ills. "The media can't do anything about that. What the media can do, however, is exacerbate or ease these worries. It all comes down to the quality of reporting on immigrant issues."

"We have all heard that sensationalism and entertainment values are on the rise in TV news," writes a Northwestern University researcher. "My studies indicate these trends aren't simply professional embarrassments and frustrations for journalists. They may also be making urban America less governable, deepening the chasm of misunderstanding and distrust between blacks and whites."

Everyone knows that bad news drives journalism, but the press disproportionately frames stories about blacks as bad news, a University of Pennsylvania media scholar finds in a pilot study he conducted. "To the extent that the media emphasize the ways in which the distribution of social and economic risks breaks down along racial lines," he suggests, "they have helped to tear us apart."

Things are looking up in terms of how the press covers America's diverse new Asian community, writes the author, a former columnist for the *Oakland Tribune*. "TV coverage of Asian Americans remains spotty and sensationalized, but print coverage, while retaining some of the old polar good-bad images, has become increasingly nuanced, textured and true to life."

Forty years after *Brown v. Board of Education,* the fight over racial segregation has flared up again, with an ironic twist—back then, blacks sued to enter white colleges; today they are fighting to keep black colleges open. "Amid the gaffes and stereotypes by the media, there has been a real dearth of relatively simple, interpretive, what-it-means reporting on the South's desegregation story," complains a Louisiana State University journalism professor.

Coverage of America's "drug wars" has been marked by racism, contend the authors of a new book on how network television reports on cocaine. "Journalism's discovery of crack in late 1985 signaled the beginning of a period of frenzied coverage in which the race and class contours of the cocaine problem established in the early 1980s would be almost completely reconfigured," they find.

Part III   Issues, Debates and Dilemmas

If *Ebony* is a "black" magazine, is the *New Republic* "white"? asks a Queens College political scientist and author. White journalists and media organizations don't see race as an essential feature of their identities, but for blacks, as the author points out, "the dominant media are most certainly white. To their eyes, the mainstream media speak for a white nation, which expects all citizens to conform to its ways."

"There is good reason for minorities to think their perspectives are at best warped by the media or, worse, not heard at all," reflect the acting communication dean at Howard University and the co-editor. "In the year that saw a black man elected president of South Africa, there is irony in the fact that apartheid still rules the information age in America."

America's image of blacks—and their own self-image—is closely tied to how they are portrayed in news and entertainment, writes the author, a former *New York Times* editor who now heads the journalism department at the University of Alabama. "There is strong objection to many of the roles and images transmitted—including the clown image of television sitcoms' 'new vaudevillians,' but particularly the messages of gangsta rappers about women as 'bitches' and 'hos,' and about guns and violence and cops."

To paraphrase the poet, What's in a name? In theory, substance should be vastly more important than labeling, but, as the co-editor points out, language questions are intensely sensitive in the arena of race in America. "Black" or "African American"? "Native American" or "Indian"? "To the extent that nit-picking over language interferes with coverage of vital racial and ethnic issues and problems, this debate may be counterproductive," he concludes. But it refuses to go away.

Part IV   A Media Industry Status Report

So far, at least, the electronic world of tomorrow looks pretty white, reflects a former broadcaster and technology expert. "Future archaeologists, studying the documentary record of the present, would have reason to conclude that people of color were bypassed by the information superhighway," he says. "Maybe it just passed over black and Latino communities, much as Manhattan's West Side Highway passes overhead on its way through Harlem neighborhoods."

"Race—it is America's rawest nerve and most enduring dilemma," reflects the author, a former newspaper editor and journalism professor at Columbia University. "From birth to death, race is with us, defining, dividing, distorting." Few social institutions are as tormented by this dilemma day in and day out as are newspapers, he says, reporting on efforts by two metropolitan dailies to come to grips with the issue.

"In the advertising world, the representation of minorities has been a topic of interest that has waxed and waned since the civil rights movement," writes a University of Illinois advertising professor. "Yet, so much has changed in the last 20 years that to view minorities in advertising solely in terms of inclusions in 'mainstream' media is to miss much of it."

"As the United States moves inexorably toward the fullness and complexity of its multicultural destiny, away from its historic Eurocentric origins, it is much easier to imagine the impact that shift will have on public institutions than to foresee what changes it holds for the ethics, standards and practices of the news media," suggests the author, executive producer of a new multicultural newsmagazine on public television.

As the U.S. Latino community grows, "newspapers can see the writing on the wall, and it's in Spanish," writes the *Chicago Tribune*'s ethnic affairs reporter in her survey of the explosion of Spanish-language newspapers published by U.S. mainstream newspapers from Chicago to Florida to California. "It was all inevitable in a society in which salsa now outsells ketchup."

Part V   Books

"Although the debate is framed in terms of participation, the real struggle over diversity in the newsroom is a conflict over points of view," observes the author, a former journalist and journalism professor at the University of Texas, in opening her critical synthesis of four key books concerning race and American media. "Eradication of racism revolves around social reconstruction and the control of representation by those denied access to media decision-making and product distribution."

Preface

Race and ethnicity are often self-consciously on the agenda of the American media. There is, of course, the matter of racial and ethnic coverage, the depiction of the nation's diverse population and their concerns. At the same time the media considers content, whether conflictual or consensual, there is also the matter of racial and ethnic representation in the media work force. While the media are clearly part of the private sector, they take on a quasipublic role in American life and have in recent years professed to represent the nation's diverse populations and concerns both through accurate and equitable news coverage and in strides toward more integrated news rooms.

This book tries to capture the essence of that process, often cast as a debate, engendering controversy and conflict. The performance of the media is under the microscope here both in how they cover minority peoples and through their concerns in public life and in connection with employment in the media and communications industries.

The Media in Black and White is a gathering together of people who know what they are talking about on these topics, either by virtue of experience in the field or in systematic research. The result is a portrait of how the media and media industries are addressing what has been called the race and ethnicity card in American life.

The material here is drawn from an issue of the *Media Studies Journal* titled "Race-America's Rawest Nerve," published at The Freedom Forum Media Studies Center at Columbia University in New York in summer 1994. That *Journal* issue debuted at Unity '94, the first-ever gathering of minority journalists—the National Association of Black Journalists, National Association of Hispanic Journalists, Asian American Journalists Association and the Native American Press Association. The issue was called "historic and courageous," by William Tatum, editor and publisher of New York's *Amsterdam News,* a leading African-American daily. Newsstand copies quickly sold out and requests to the Media Studies Center depleted supplies. Later, university courses in media studies, ethnic studies and other fields adopted the *Journal* as a text. That demand lead to this book.

When the *Journal* was published and the book put in press it was my pleasure to be editor-in-chief of the *Media Studies Journal* and executive director of the Media Studies Center. In that capacity I worked closely with editor Edward Pease, now at Utah State University, whose contributions to the *Journal,* including a co-authored chapter, are gratefully acknowledged. Also deserving of many kudos are Lisa DeLisle of the *Journal* staff, my superb assistant Cate Dolan, who quietly coordinated many matters connected to the *Journal,* and my current administrative assistant, Stephan Wilson.

After nearly two centuries of coverage marked by demeaning depictions, discrimination or neglect, America's majority media, virtually all white-owned, from the 1960s forward adopted an official policy that has been characterized by some as "catch-up and concern." Since the time of the seminal 1968 Kerner Commission report—a document that boldly declared that the United States was not one, but two societies, "one black, one white, separate and unequal," media industry organizations, professional societies, journalism schools and human rights groups have made representative coverage of the minority community and better representation in the media work force matters of conscious policy. Concurrently, the minority media groups previously mentioned gave voice to individuals eager to play a role in media operations, first as employees, later as managers and with the hope of executive and ownership venues. Other related press organizations sounded volleys in the ownership battles, which continue as this is written.

In some sleepy quarters, people benignly asked why all the fuss, or expressed resentment at what they saw as a backlash response, but the reasons were abundantly clear for all but the most obtuse observers. Whatever the conditions of people elsewhere on the globe in settings also known for racial and ethnic hatred and discrimination, the American experience with Indian genocide and repression, with blacks and slavery, with "yellow peril" attacks on Asians and mean-spirited discrimination against Hispanics or Latinos graphically answered the question. The legacy of discrimination and raw race relations was itself enough of a reason for modern media, whether in information and opinion or in entertainment or advertising, to pay more attention to race, both as the sustenance for content and in connection with the people who work in, run, own and operate media organizations and institutions. But this was not simply a matter of fairness and equity to once-scorned and ignored racial minority groups; it was also good business, recognizing that, collectively, minorities were becoming a more and more vital part of the nation's population and the media audience.

Indeed, the minority population in the United States today constitutes almost 25 percent of the total, which demographers say will grow to more than half the population by 2060. Thus, within three generations, today's collective "minority" will be the majority and, perhaps more importantly, in the short run they are distinctive portions of the population with cultural and, increasingly, political clout. German-Americans may be the largest ethnic minority in the country today, but they have long since forsaken any serious and visible unified public identity. The same is true with many other European-American ethnic groups who, like today's racial minorities, also once were shunned, caricatured and marginalized. Claims about the coming new "majority" ought not be overstated, however. Demographers point out that well into the second half of the next century whites will still be the largest single racial group and also that many persons with Hispanic surnames consider themselves white. The notion of the groups currently called racial and ethnic minorities becoming the majority presumes some common "people of color" identity and some wherewithal to work together toward common ends. Otherwise this new majority of such great promise for true diversity could be squandered.

While the term "race"—meaning, in the words of the *American Heritage Dictionary of the English Language,* "a local geographic or global human population distinguished as a more or less distinct group by genetically transmitted physical characteristics"—was once used more generally to describe any people who had a "common history, nationality or distribution," it has come to be mostly associated with color in the late twentieth century. In the United States, that means African Americans or blacks, Hispanics or Latinos, Native Americans or Indians and Asian Americans. For social scientists there is "remarkable international consensus that race implies common descent, matched by an enormous confusion...about what common descent implies," according to the *Dictionary of the Social Sciences.* Clearly, race is most commonly associated with "race and minority group relations," usually, but not always, involving color.

As Sig Gissler, former editor of the *Milwaukee Journal* and now a journalism professor at Columbia University declares, "race is America's rawest nerve." He and other leading journalists should know, since race has so often dominated the news, whether in connection with civil unrest, class, crime or achievement. So has the depiction of minority group members in the news, in entertainment programs and advertising—not to mention textbooks, outdoor advertising and other media forms—been the subject of much contemporary debate. While media content about this "rawest nerve" has too often been predominantly negative, both in terms of portrayals and coverage, the media have at the same time made good-faith efforts to cover minority issues fairly and sensitively.

Take almost any issue involving a person who happens to be "nonwhite" (the truly colorless moniker given to the massive multicultural polyglot that makes up the minority population), and race is on the agenda. As this book was being prepared, colossal media coverage focused on O.J. Simpson, a double murder and a prime-time televised car chase along 60 miles of Los Angeles freeway. Interestingly, the story didn't take on racial overtones—even though Simpson is black and the murder victims were white—until *Time* magazine ran a doctored police mugshot of Simpson on its cover. Critics unleashed what *Time* managing editor James R. Gaines called a "storm of controversy"—by darkening Simpson's face, they complained, the news magazine effectively was sending him "back to the ghetto." Then NAACP head Benjamin Chavis said *Time* presented Simpson as "some kind of animal, sinister and criminal." Although magazines and other media commonly manipulate other images, especially that of the president, this one immediately ignited controversy. "What's wrong with this picture?" wondered the *Washington Post*. It was, some critics argued, "racist, pure and simple."

One television panel featuring the Reverend Jesse Jackson argued that blacks involved in sexual controversies become the lightening rod for coverage that links them to unsavory activities, whether sexual harassment in case of allegations against Justice Clarence Thomas, child sexual abuse charges involving rock singer Michael Jackson, the rape conviction of boxer Mike Tyson or spousal abuse in the instance of O.J. Simpson. While this is no doubt true, the same thing happens when any celebrity is connected with the unusual, bizarre or the untoward. But in the wake of so many years of unfair frontal assaults, African Americans and other groups are understandably and justifiably sensitive to negative portrayals that move from the specific to the general with such speed. Ironically, Simpson, whose fame was widespread before his arrest, rarely was associated with news *per se*. His public persona developed in college and professional sports, and spread to movies and advertising. He had, in fact, traversed virtually all of the media functions, with limited exposure as a pure news figure until the tragedies of June 1994. The Simpson trial, which eventually ended in an acquittal in October 1995, is already the subject of several books, dominated the news for more than a year and became perhaps the most race-sensitive news story of all times. It continues to be the cause of much racial and ethnic polarization.

It is the legacy of neglect and negative portrayal that makes humor involving members of minority groups all but impossible, as it does with certain ethnic minorities. Since caricature is by definition unfair, trafficking as it does in stereotypes and exaggeration of physical features, the raw nerves associated with race immediately retract, fearful that commentary and comedic depictions not intended to denigrate and demean, might do so anyway. Nowhere is this more evident than in situation comedies on television, which have handled racial humor best in programs dominated by minority persons, such as "The Cosby Show." Norman Lear's efforts in the 1970s to attack bigotry in his program "All in the Family" featured an offensive but "lovable" bigot, Archie Bunker, spouting things that were commonly said in daily parlance, but not in public media. The result, some researchers said, was not the breaking down of racial barriers but the reinforcement of them. People who were already tolerant and open laughed and enjoyed the program as the satire it was intended, while others who truly identified with Archie cheered his bigoted opinions.

All this means that the long journey wherein media and race are comfortable companions is still just beginning. This book, with its emphasis on the current interface between media and race, is an effort to move another step toward understanding, mutual respect and possible solutions to matters much discussed and less often satisfactorily resolved.

This examination of *The Media in Black and White* brings together twenty journalists and scholars—of various racial backgrounds—to grapple with a common, thorny issue: the role that media industries from advertising to newspapers to the information superhighway play in helping Americans understand race.

Two essays begin the process of "Reviewing the American Melting Pot." First, *Newsweek*'s Ellis Close discusses the various ways race plays in the newsrooms and performance of U.S. news organizations in "Seeth-

xvi   The Media in Black and White

ing in Silence—The News in Black and White." "Is objectivity (or even fairness) possible when dealing with people from different racial groups and cultural backgrounds?" he wonders. "Can any of us be trusted to make sense of lives essentially alien to our own? Does 'getting it right' mean anything more virtuous than conforming to prevailing prejudice?" In response, Manning Marable, director of Columbia University's African-American research center, observes in "Reconciling Race and Reality" that such hopes are long shots, but worth holding. Despite what he calls the "unambiguously negative" 1990s in U.S. race relations, and the fact that "few of us—black or white—really want to discuss the root causes of America's parallel universe," Marable says the media may offer the best available tool for fulfilling Martin Luther King Jr.'s 1963 dream of equality and understanding.

Seven authors then combine to examine media performance in a section titled "Covering America." John J. Miller, associate director of the Manhattan Institute's Center for the New American Community in Washington, opens with a salvo at what he sees as a flourishing new strain of American racism in his essay, "Immigration, the Press and the New Racism." Governors of four states have sued the federal government to recover costs of illegal immigration, he reflects; New York's World Trade Center bombing focused on immigrants, and then there was the case of Zoe Baird's immigrant nanny and the shipwreck of the Golden Venture with hundreds of Chinese aboard. "Whenever immigrants make the news these days, it seems it's always bad news."

From Northwestern University, media researcher Robert M. Entman discusses his studies of television in "African Americans According to TV News." And the news is not good. "The choices TV journalists make appear to feed racial stereotypes, encouraging white hostility and fear of African Americans," he reports. "TV news, especially local news, paints a picture of blacks as violent and threatening toward whites." That fits with what the University of Pennsylvania's Oscar H. Gandy, Jr. found in his study of the way newspapers frame news about African Americans. In "From Bad to Worse—The Media's Framing of Race and Risk," Gandy writes that because news about blacks is so often framed in the negative, the media help create a false public perception of African Americans.

Not all the news is bad, however, as newspaper columnist William Wong observes in "Covering the Invisible 'Model Minority.'" He writes, "Not all that long ago, Asian Americans could rightly complain that mainstream news media either ignored them or covered them in shallow, stereotypical ways." But a broader worldview and more Asian Americans in the news media work force have resulted in more sensitive and informed coverage, Wong says. Meanwhile, in the South, an ironic twist in the old story of racial desegregation in higher education has pointed up some consistent failings in the press, reports Dale Thom, a Louisiana State University journalism professor. In his essay, "In the South—Press, Courts and Desegregation revisited," Thom says the media have missed the boat in covering school issues in nineteen states whose laws once required racially separate colleges. This section concludes with a piece from Jimmie L. Reeves and Richard Campbell, authors of a book on how television covered race and America's drug wars. In "Coloring the Crack Crisis," the two researchers reveal that when cocaine was seen as a recreational drug used by white yuppies, the networks portrayed drug crimes much differently than they did when cocaine gave way to crack, an evil substance associated with poor people of color in the inner city. "The crack crisis helped promote a new racist backlash that justified the symbolic criminalization of a generation of black youth," they write.

The book's third section examines "Issues, Debates and Dilemmas" affecting the interaction of race and the mass media. Author Andrew Hacker leads off with a reflective essay that wonders, "Are the Media Really 'White'?" It's a matter of whom you ask. "The mainstream media, like other major institutions, reject any racial label as irrelevant and inappropriate," Hacker observes. "Why, they might ask, should race be seen as the central feature of diverse media systems and complex personalities?"

The impact of such denial of race consciousness within organizational attitudes in the media also has the effect of "Warping the World," suggest Howard University's Jannette L. Dates and journalism educator Edward C. Pease in an essay subtitled "Media's Mangled Images of Race." They write, "The norm in this country is that the perspectives of white, mainstream men create the lenses through which America—whether peripherally or directly—views race, and itself." And the skewed images thus created, continues Paul Delaney of the University of Alabama, negatively affect how whites see blacks in this country, and how blacks see themselves. In "Pop Culture, 'Gangsta Rap' and the 'New Vaudeville,'" Delaney complains about sitcom portrayals of blacks as clowns, and rappers' pathological view of women and violence.

The editor of this volume concludes this section with a look at "Racial Naming" and the delicate and frequently hurtful nuances of how we refer to one another. "The tortured history of racial, religious and ethnic name-calling in America makes clear the pain and pleasure associated with racial and ethnic monikers," he reflects.

Next comes a selective "Media Industry Status Report" on how race plays in various media businesses. Adam Clayton Powell III, a former television and radio executive, now a vice president for technology at The Freedom Forum, examines "On-Ramps to the Information Super-highway" and questions of access and content diversity in the electronic future. "Industry groups and government policymakers mirror today's consumers of news media: Data indicate those new media consumers are disproportionately white and male," he says.

From new media to old, race issues pose similarly difficult problems for media gatekeepers. In "Newspapers' Quest for Racial Candor," former *Milwaukee Journal* editor Sig Gissler reflects on what he learned in his research on media and ethnic coverage. "America's rawest nerve and most enduring dilemma," race divides both the society and the media institutions that cover it, Gissler says, reporting on two newspapers that confronted race issues directly.

From news we move to advertising, and University of Illinois advertising professor Lisa Peñaloza's view of how U.S. businesses are discovering the Latino consumer market. In "Ya Viene Atzlan! Latinos in U.S. Advertising," Peñazola provides some insights into advertisers' motivations in their new interest for Spanish-speaking audiences. Meanwhile, public television producer John Phillip Santos issues a call for a new, fuller media depiction of American diversity. In "(Re)Imagining America," Santos offers a prescription for a new brand of coverage that truly reflects the nation. "The long-hallowed cult of journalistic 'objectivity' has too often been a veneer for what is essentially a predominating white male point of view in our news culture," he reflects. "But in terms of journalism education and technique, what do we put in its place?" One other new approach to increasing multiculturalism in mainstream media is described in " Hola, America! Newsstand 2000," in which *Chicago Tribune* ethnic affairs writer Melita Marie Garza reviews the growth and impact of Spanish-language newspapers. "Between 1990 and 1993, the nation's Latino community grew more than any other group, jumping from 22.4 million to 25.1 million, an increase of almost a million a year," she observes. "So it's little wonder that the major media developed a mania for the Spanish-language market."

Finally, University of Texas journalism professor Mercedes Lynn de Uriarte provides the endpoint to this treatment of race and media with a book review essay titled "Exploring (and Exploding) the U.S. Media Prism." In considering four major books that examine various facets of the media-race relationship, de Uriarte reports critically on the debate concerning race in media content, workplaces and coverage. The media view the world, she says, through a "prism of hegemony," a perspective that distorts and marginalizes minority viewpoints and offers a one-eyed vision.

It is our hope that these authors and their perspectives can broaden a one-eyed vision of the United States and the world beyond. In the wake of racial riots that scarred U.S. cities in the 1960s, the Kerner Commission outlined the problem with clarity:

> Our fundamental criticism is that the news media have failed to analyze and report adequately on racial problems in the United States and, as a related matter, to meet the Negro's legitimate expectations of journalism.... The media write and report from the standpoint of a white man's world.... Slights and indignities are part of the Negro's daily life, and many of them come from what he now calls the "white press"—a press that repeatedly, if unconsciously, reflects the biases, the paternalism, the indifference of white America. This may be understandable, but it is not excusable in an institution that has the mission to inform and educate the whole of our society.

Expanded in 1996—when one quarter of U.S. society is minority—to include all ethnic and racial minority groups and all media, this indictment is still on target.

Everette E. Dennis
March 1996

America's Rawest Nerve

I

Reviewing the American Melting Pot

1

Seething in Silence—
The News in Black and White

Ellis Cose

For reporters, race can be a treacherous subject, raising questions that go to the heart of the journalist's craft. Is objectivity (or even fairness) possible when dealing with people from different racial groups and cultural backgrounds? Can any of us be trusted to make sense of lives essentially alien to our own? Does "getting it right" mean anything more virtuous than conforming to prevailing prejudice?

Journalists are inclined to believe that a good eye and an unbiased heart can ensure essential accuracy, regardless of the personal (or racial) baggage one brings to the table. Yet as Ben Bagdikian notes in his classic *The Media Monopoly,* "News, like all human observations, is not truly objective.... Human scenes described by different individuals are seen with differences." Arguably, no differences loom larger than those connected with ethnicity and race.

Anyone doubting the polarizing potential of race in America (and beyond) need look no farther than the typical American newsroom. Last year, in attempting to assess the impact of race on American lives, the *Akron Beacon Journal* also took a look at itself. With nine white and eight black journalists, the paper formed two separate focus groups. What it quickly discovered was that although all of the participants worked at the same institution, they saw it quite differently. The blacks, by and large, believed that the deck was stacked against them. Despite the fact that the publisher was an African American, many felt that the real control resided in the hands of whites who understood neither them nor their community.

3

In contrast, the white journalists at the *Beacon Journal* felt that blacks (and black issues) were receiving special treatment. As the paper's 1994 Pulitzer Prize-winning report observed, whites at the paper felt a "constant pressure...to bend over backward to embrace minority perspectives." Indeed, anxiety among whites seemed even higher than among blacks. And practically everyone—regardless of race—seemed fearful of speaking their minds. Whites feared being censured as politically incorrect; blacks fretted over repercussions that might affect their careers if they dared to complain about racism.

Responses of focus groups comprised of ordinary citizens were strikingly similar to those of the journalists. The *Beacon Journal* found that while blacks saw racism as a constant in their lives, whites felt that racism (especially institutional racism) had largely been eliminated. The paper also discovered that people had a hard time talking honestly about race, and everyone—regardless of race—seemed troubled and frustrated by the pressures that race questions imposed on their lives. As the *Beacon Journal* report put it, "Whites are tired of hearing about it. Blacks wish it would go away. All seem powerless to move it." The paper went on to observe, "The typical white American will go to great lengths simply to avoid the subject. And that skittishness may be getting in the way of solutions."

Journalists, of course, are supposed to be different from ordinary citizens, at least when it comes to confronting difficult truths. But race, it seems, can make cowards of us all. It is not merely cowardice, however, that makes honest racial dialogue difficult. The difficulty also derives from the fact that perceptions vary radically as a function of race—or, more accurately, as a function of the very different experiences members of various racial groups have endured.

In the past two years (since the massive riots in Los Angeles), a number of major newspapers have produced impressive in-depth reports on race relations in America. The narratives are uniformly somber and, in some respects, dispiriting. The *Chicago Sun-Times* focused on what it called the "great divide," and presented an extensive poll documenting just how wide that divide has become. The *Indianapolis Star*, sounding a similar theme, quoted a local minister who said, "There are no race relations. We are two different communities in two different worlds that hardly have anything to do with each other."

In its seven-month series, the *Times-Picayune* of New Orleans traced American (and its own city's) race relations from slavery to modern times and concluded with a forceful and sober editorial:

We live separately. Worship separately. We stand apart, frozen that way by the mythical but overpowering thing called race, America's arbitrary, color-coded system of defining, dividing and oppressing. It is a painful fact, so much so that we can scarcely talk about it. But we must.

During the past seven months, the *Times-Picayune* has tried to do that with its series "Together Apart: The Myth of Race." We have done so with the abiding belief that our quality of life and the very future of our community depend on that dialogue.... Through two years of research, hundreds of interviews, dozens of stories and pictures and thousands of callers' comments, this newspaper has tried to show that any meaningful solution we might propose...must begin with a simple, yet monumental conversation.

The editorial went on to observe and confess: "It's a queasy undertaking, talking about race. Especially when your own house is not in order." Indeed, as the *Times-Picayune* worked through the questions raised by the series, it found its own staff to be a microcosm of the divisions it detailed in greater New Orleans. In order to help it resolve the difficult internal issues, the newspaper brought in outside "diversity" experts to work intensively with its newsroom staff. Sig Gissler, a Freedom Forum Media Studies Center senior fellow who examined the *Times-Picayune* case, likens the process to an organization going into exhaustive group psychotherapy.

Few news organizations are prepared to go to the trouble and expense of putting their staffs on the equivalent of a psychiatrist's couch. Yet, without some artificial form of intervention, America's newsrooms seem destined to remain divided along racial lines.

In an attempt to explore life across those lines, the *Indianapolis Star* sent several black and white reporters into places or situations where persons of their race were not normally found. Some reporters went on interracial "dates." Some visited each other's homes, an experience that led one white reporter, Bill Theobald, to admit, "My views about race have mostly been formed by thinking, by reading or by talking to whites. Talking to blacks about the subject is uncomfortable. I don't know how to ask the questions; perhaps I am afraid of the answers."

Such soul-searching was doubtlessly healthy for the *Star,* but the fact that it took a newspaper series to get veteran journalists to emerge from their cocoons is not exactly reassuring. Yet Theobald's relative racial isolation appears to be the norm in the news business, and that isolation goes a long way toward explaining why the perspectives of black and white journalists are often very far apart.

The National Association of Black Journalists' 1993 *Muted Voices* study was in large measure a testimonial to the existence of that perceptual gap. The survey of the NABJ members and white managers found that the two groups see the world from such different vantage points that it is difficult to believe they work in the same industry, much less in the same newsrooms. Seventy-three percent of the NABJ members polled thought blacks were less likely than other journalists to advance; only 2 percent of the white managers felt that way. Most of the black journalists surveyed thought blacks were forced to spend more time than whites in entry-level positions. Only 2 percent of the managers thought so. Question after question yielded similar results, and although the NABJ survey compared white management to black staffers, it's a good bet that much the same would have been found if the researchers had polled whites and blacks of more equal status.

A 1991 Ohio University job-satisfaction survey found that white journalists, by and large, believed that whites were at a significant disadvantage in newsrooms. Two-thirds of the white respondents thought minorities received preferential treatment, and one-third believed that minorities received more opportunities than whites.

"At the present time, my newspaper discriminates on the basis of race and sex," one respondent wrote. "White males need not apply or expect to be treated the same as others in the newsroom."

As the poll clearly documents, the sense of disadvantage among white journalists is widespread, even as minority journalists continue to complain that they are the ones discriminated against—though these complaints, typically, are not voiced aloud. The NABJ survey found, for instance, that one-third of the black respondents were afraid to raise racial issues out of fear that to do so would damage their careers.

A decade ago, management consultant Edward W. Jones conducted a massive three-year research project looking at blacks in corporate America and published the results in a 1986 article in the *Harvard Business Review*. Like NABJ's pollsters, Jones found an overwhelming sense among blacks that life, for them, was grossly unfair: 98 percent said that subtle prejudice pervaded their companies, and 90 percent reported a "climate of support" worse than that for their white peers. Eighty-four percent said that their race had worked to their disadvantage when it came to ratings, pay, assignments, recognition, appraisals and promotion. Fewer than 10 percent reported an atmosphere at work in which open discussion of racial issues was promoted. Conversely, when Jones talked to white management at the firms, he found that whites saw a markedly different picture: Indeed, they saw their firms as bastions of tolerance, places that were essentially color-blind.

Jones threw his hands up at the perceptual discrepancies, concluding that regardless of whose perceptions were correct "by some impossible objective standard," the corporations had a serious problem. When I spoke with him in 1992 while conducting research for my book *The Rage of a Privileged Class,* he had concluded that the workplace race situation was worse than ever: Blacks in corporations were not only still suffering but "some of us are losing hope," he said. "The psychological casualty rate is very high."

It's impossible to calculate the magnitude of any "psychological casualty rate." What is obvious, however, is that muting expression carries a price, not only psychologically, but journalistically. Moreover, as management consultant Jones says, "How the heck do we solve something we can't talk about?"

Yet, if the results of the myriad focus groups, surveys and private testimony that have been conducted on this issue are to be believed, journalists are fearful of honesty. The image of journalists as reticent, fearful communicators doesn't easily square with the stereotype of loud-mouthed reporters unafraid of saying whatever pops into their head. Yet, if neither white nor black journalists feel comfortable talking about race, it's unlikely that preconceptions will be seriously questioned in the press, and it's inevitable that racial coverage will be driven largely by timorousness or hackneyed tradition.

In this age of political correctness, complaints of timid coverage are not difficult to find, whether it's white journalists griping about having to cater to minorities in Akron, or conservatives accusing the *New York Times* of being overly respectful of gays. Yet, even if we assume the complaints are valid, the conventional approach to racial coverage is not a satisfactory alternative. For conventional coverage, as a number of researchers have shown, tends to disparage minorities.

Robert Entman of Northwestern University, for instance, notes that a disproportionate share of TV news and reality-based programming depicts minorities in stereotypical ways. Large numbers of African Americans and Latinos, he says, are cast as victims or victimizers of society, but few (in contrast to whites) are pictured as productive citizens.

The preponderance of such images, argues Entman, may have serious effects. For, in a country that remains largely segregated, whites' notions of what it means to be black and Latino are derived largely from what they see on television. And the picture they get, claims Entman, is of an inner city "dominated by dangerous and irresponsible minorities." In his analysis of coverage in the Chicago area, Entman found that white victims of crime were given more airtime than black victims; yet black assailants were given more extensive coverage than their numbers merited. The result, says Entman, is a picture of a society "in which minorities, especially blacks and to a lesser extent Latinos, play a heavy role in causing violence but make little contribution toward helping society cope with it."

Looking over Entman's research took me back to my days as a young writer and reporter for the *Chicago Sun-Times*. Late one Saturday night I was in the newsroom when word of a murder came from the reporter at police headquarters. Upon hearing the sketchy details, the man who was working the city desk slot hollered back to the rewrite man taking the reporter's call, "Is it a good address?"

No one in the newsroom had to ask what that question meant. We all understood that a good address was one that was affluent and white—perhaps on Chicago's Gold Coast, or in one of its ritzier suburbs. It went without saying that a tragedy in such a community was worth more ink than a tragedy in one that was not white and not wealthy. I don't recall the answer to the slot man's question, but the question itself has haunted me for some 20 years, for it sums up an essential part of conventional journalism's point of view.

Today, though we live in a world (as we constantly remind ourselves) that is increasingly multicultural, much of conventional journalism remains fixated on the lives of the white and the wealthy. I was reminded of that in 1994, when one of my issues of *New York* magazine arrived. It featured an article that purported to identify the best places to find any number of products and services one might search for in New York City. I was struck by the fact that in a city that is a virtual United Nations—it is said that more than 119 languages and dialects are spoken in New York—practically every face attached to the magazine's recommendations was white. Clearly, New York, as viewed by the magazine's editors, remains a very white place.

The alternative to such one-sided coverage need not necessarily amount to twisting the news into a politically correct caricature of reality. But achieving better and more balanced journalism ultimately depends on having journalists who are wise enough and varied enough to see the world in its true complexity. Certainly, the news world is closer to that ideal than it was in, say, 1978. That was the year when the American Society of Newspaper Editors pledged that the industry's newsroom demographics would mirror the country's by the end of the century.

Every year since then, ASNE has compiled statistics that show slow progress toward that goal (albeit, not enough progress to provide much hope that it will be reached). Most recently, the percentage of minority journalists in U.S. newspaper newsrooms was computed at 10.49. (The U.S. population is approaching 25 percent minority.) At certain large papers, the percentage is considerably higher: Just over 17 percent of the newsroom work force at newspapers of over 500,000 daily circulation are members of minority groups, as were 24 percent of all first-time journalist hires and 39 percent of newsroom interns over the last year.

That some segments of the newspaper industry take the diversity effort seriously is apparent not only from the new hiring statistics, but from the high-profile involvement of the Newspaper Association of America. In January 1992, the American Newspaper Publishers Association (now the Newspaper Association of America) brought together the heads of several of the nation's biggest newspaper companies. Summit conveners named a host of committees to work on various aspects of diversity. They also embraced (and broadened) ASNE's hiring goals, encouraging newspapers to achieve "work force parity with respect to women and minorities within their markets, including all levels of management, by the year 2000 or sooner."

As with ASNE, however, the NAA has been plagued by questions about the seriousness of its quest and about the odds of success. At a second summit meeting in December of 1992, James Batten, chairman of Knight-Ridder Inc., grappled with those questions. "I think we all understand that NAA is not in a position to compel anybody to do anything," he said. "Our power, to the degree that we have power, comes from our ability to experiment, our ability to persuade. It comes from our ability to encourage, to educate, with maybe a touch of inspiration here and there."

It was probably as good an answer as he could have given. For the fact is that, for all the activity around the summits, NAA and the other industry organizations don't have the final word. What ultimately happens in newsrooms across America has much less to do with what NAA (or any trade organization) says than with what a myriad of individual editors and publishers decide. Setting industry goals is primarily an exercise in symbolism. This is not to say that taking such a stand doesn't have an impact. It does. Among other things, it serves to legitimize the goal of newsroom integration. And, though newspapers are far from seeing the goals achieved, they are further along that route than the other major players in the news business. Television, outside major urban areas, is not a particularly integrated enterprise. And mainstream magazine staffs remain, for the most part, overwhelmingly white.

Yet, for all the attention annually focused on ASNE's numbers and other industry statistics tracking progress, news organizations must ultimately be judged less on the composition of their staffs then on the composition of their front pages and broadcasts. Clearly, a direct relationship exists between staffing and the news reported, but to concentrate only on hiring statistics is to lose sight of the larger issues. For even if newspapers can manage to achieve demographic parity with the general population, that alone will not guarantee a more honest and representative brand of reporting. The problem lies as much in our attitudes as in our statistics.

As the *Muted Voices* study and the *Akron Beacon Journal*'s report make clear, attitudes in the newsroom are much like those in the world we cover. To some extent, that will always be the case. For journalists cannot afford to cut themselves off from their surroundings. Yet, neither can they afford to allow racial anxieties to take precedence over honest effective communication. For if we remain ignorant of how to ask questions or afraid of the answers those questions might provoke, we will also remain inadequate to the task of covering the news.

Ellis Cose is a contributing editor at Newsweek *and author of* The Press *(1989),* A Nation of Strangers *(1992), and* The Rage of a Privileged Class *(1993).*

2

Reconciling Race and Reality

Manning Marable

A generation has passed since Martin Luther King Jr. stood on the steps of the Lincoln Memorial on Aug. 28, 1963, and declared, "I have a dream," a speech that forever changed the lives not only of the quarter-million Americans who had gathered in Washington's hot afternoon sun, but the lives of Americans everywhere. It was the largest single demonstration in U.S. history up to that time, people who came to support passage of a civil rights bill that had been stalled in the Senate. Motivated by a deep belief in the possibility of racial integration, the idea that Negro Americans would one day achieve political, economic and social opportunities within the mainstream of American society, they were convinced that racial inequality could be uprooted by changing the laws that regulated public behavior and social relations. They genuinely believed that America's future would be more equitable for racial minorities than its past had been.

In the more than 30 years since the zenith of this Second Reconstruction, Americans have experienced what I have termed a "paradox of desegregation." Laws restricting the social equality of African Americans were indeed abolished—the Voting Rights Act of 1965 extended the electoral franchise to millions of Southern blacks. Since 1964, the number of black elected officials has increased dramatically, from barely 100 when King made his historic speech, to about 8,000 today; in that time, the number of African-American mayors has increased from zero to nearly 400. In economic terms, the size of the black consumer market also has soared, from approximately $30 billion a year in spending nationally in 1964 to $270 billion in 1993. During these years, the size of the African-

11

American middle class has quadrupled; by 1990, one black household out of seven recorded an annual income of $50,000 or more.

These statistical symbols of racial success and upward mobility notwithstanding, the trend in U.S. race relations in the 1990s has been unambiguously negative. Despite passage of desegregationist legislation and the accelerated growth of a black middle class, a growing pessimism pervades American public discourse and perspectives along the color line. Ironically, today's worst racial divisions appear among young Americans under the age of 25.

An October 1991 nationwide poll of 15- to 24-year-olds by Peter D. Hart Research Associates uncovered disturbing trends in their racial beliefs and perceptions among young American whites. When asked if colleges should give "special considerations" to recruiting and admitting students of color, 51 percent of young whites said no. Two-thirds of all young whites would disapprove of businesses that give "special consideration to minority job applicants." And 78 percent of young whites said businesses should not extend "special preference" in evaluating minority job applicants.

The figures indicate that many young white Americans feel threatened by diversity and believe that white racism no longer exists—for them, the chief victims of discrimination are white, not black. Indeed, when asked whether "discrimination was more likely to hurt a white or minority person seeking scholarships, jobs or promotions," 49 percent of whites said they "were more likely to lose out" than minorities. In contrast, 68 percent of young African Americans, 52 percent of Latinos, but only 34 percent of the whites believed that "minorities were more likely to lose." About half of all young Americans polled characterized race relations as "generally bad."

On U.S. college campuses, many white students believe that less qualified minorities are displacing more qualified whites as faculty and administrators. But according to a recent Carnegie Commission educational report, when levels of educational attainment and scholarly productivity are equivalent, African-American professors receive tenure and promotion at lower rates than whites, who hold 87 percent of all tenure-track faculty positions at American universities.

Meanwhile, white students complain that affirmative action policies bring "unqualified" students of color into their colleges and classrooms. But few of them discuss university "legacy" policies, college practices of admitting the sons, daughters and grandchildren of alumni, even when their academic records may be less than competitive. At Harvard, for example, the general admissions rate for "legacies" in 1992 was 44 percent.

One myth circulating holds that hundreds of thousands of Latino, Native American and African-American students are taking college opportunities away from whites. But the reality is that during the 1980s, the percentage of minority high school graduates who went to college declined. In 1975, about 36 percent of all Latino high school graduates aged 18 to 26 were enrolled in college; by 1988, only 26.8 percent in this age group were in school. A similar retreat from educational equality occurred among black students during the period: 32 percent were in college in 1975, compared to 28.1 percent in 1988. At the same time, the percentage of white high school graduates going to college rose from 32.4 percent in 1975 to 38.1 percent in 1988.

Meanwhile, racial divisions are widening on the streets of America. I've witnessed this scene myself many times: As young blacks or Latinos walk into a store, security guards nervously shadow them. As they walk toward the cash register and the checkout line, white matrons grip their purses tighter. Video cameras record every step until the teen-agers leave the store.

White Americans refuse to talk honestly about their racial anxieties and prejudices, or about the not-too-subtle changes in their behavior when they are confronted by a person of color. Much of what white, middle-class America knows about black America is learned from television and films where, for generations, African Americans have been depicted as oversexed maniacs, crack-smoking criminals, dumb athletes and Aunt Jemimas, as lazy, shiftless, ignorant and hopeless.

In recent years, however, television has added a new level of pathology to the white mind's popular image of blackness. Contrary to the pathology projected by the popular media, the vast majority of black people have little tolerance for crime and violence—blacks understand all too well that we are their principal victims. But so many TV programs and major films automatically focus on that tiny fraction of the African-American community that engages in drugs and violence. Most African-American inner-city residents are not drug dealers or criminals, contrary to the impression promoted by American media.

"As long as it's in the ghetto and people are carrying guns and even the dogs speak in four-letter words, they'll give it four thumbs up and nine stars," says black comedian/director Robert Townsend. The reality of race in America aside, white film executives say, "Give us the ugliest side of the world." Charles S. Dutton, star of the TV series "Roc," points out, "If the kids who made *Menace II Society* had gone to a studio and said that they wanted to make a movie called *Contributors II Society* about black kids going to college, it would never have been made."

Media images of African Americans aside, most of us work for a living. The majority of Americans who are on welfare and Aid to Families with Dependent Children aren't black, they're white. Most of those Americans who consume cocaine and other illegal narcotics also are white, not black, not Latino. There are black criminals, of course, but most black people are not—they struggle to keep their households together, raise their children with love and attention—they are responsible and hardworking people. That is seldom the image we see of ourselves in popular American culture, particularly on television.

When the reality of blackness contradicts the stereotype of racism, TV producers, directors and corporate executives demand that reality conform to their prejudices. When black film director Kevin Hooks shot a park scene in Harlem, his studio's white executives wanted more trash, filth and litter dumped onto the set—Harlem was simply "too clean" for white folks to accept for the purposes of the movie.

How deeply rooted are racial stereotypes? In 1993, the National Science Foundation funded a national survey of more than 2,200 American adults designed to measure their racial attitudes. The study's directors, including Stanford University political scientist Paul Sniderman and University of California at Berkeley professors Philip Tetlock and Anthony Tyler, said "the most striking result" of their survey "is the sheer frequency with which negative characterizations of blacks are quite openly expressed throughout the white general population." Not surprisingly, respondents identifying themselves as white and conservative had little reluctance in expressing prejudices about African Americans. But what surprised researchers was the deep racial hostility expressed by white liberals.

For example, says Sniderman, 51 percent of the white conservatives agreed that "blacks are aggressive or violent," and so did 45 percent of the white liberals. Thirty-four percent of conservatives and 19 percent of liberals agreed that "blacks are lazy"; 21 percent of white conservatives and 17 percent of liberals concurred that African Americans are "irresponsible." And the researchers found little difference in the policy preferences of white conservative Republicans and liberal Democrats who expressed intolerant views of blacks, which may explain why it is so difficult for Congress to enact meaningful legislation that addresses the inequality and discrimination that black people face every day. White liberals dislike blacks almost as much as white conservatives do.

How to explain such persistent racism in American life? Nobel Laureate Toni Morrison sees race as "hidden and covert," obscured from the light of a frank and honest analysis. Rather than using overtly racist epithets, Americans who believe in the inferiority of people of color rely on "code words" and subtle innuendoes to justify discrimination.

But the dilemma goes deeper than prejudicial language or attitudes. The burden of discrimination is translated into radically different perceptions of the world, which separate white upper- and middle-class America from the vast majority of black, brown and poor people. This division even transcends the racial bifurcation outlined by the 1968 report of the Kerner Commission, which warned that America was rapidly becoming two unequal societies, one black and one white. A more accurate description of our current racial impasse is to speak of two "parallel universes," in which individuals and groups cohabit the same social, political and cultural space, but perceive the world in sharply divergent ways.

Black urban residents, for example, have known for decades about "redlining," the bank practice of systematically rejecting loan applications from black and Latino neighborhoods. Such policies are reinforced by the property insurance industry, which routinely rejects a much higher percentage of minority applications for insurance than whites. According to the research of the Association for Community Organizations for Reform Now (ACORN), this discrimination forms a nationwide pattern.

In Milwaukee, for example, 30 percent of all single-family homes owned by low-income African Americans are insured, compared to 79 percent of all similar dwellings owned by low-income whites. In Minneapolis, 48 percent of the black single-family homes are insured vs. 80 percent of the homes in comparable white neighborhoods. ACORN also discovered that African Americans and Latinos invariably pay much higher rates than whites to insure homes of identical value. In Kansas City, for example, ACORN found that minorities pay .88 percent of their home's value in low-income minority neighborhoods, while white homeowners in comparable white low-income communities pay about half as much—.45 percent of their home's value. The reality, which most whites don't see, is that blacks pay more and receive less for comparable goods and services. Where is the press coverage of this story?

Blacks experience the greatest discrimination in rural areas, where black farm families are on the brink of extinction. An Associated Press analysis of the records of the Farmers' Home Administration during the Reagan and Bush years found that black farmers received a loan average of 51 cents on every dollar loaned to white-owned farms. In 1992, African-American farmers in Mississippi and Alabama filed a petition charging that the FHA had "refused to respond to reports of blatant race discrimination" by their officials. But there has been little media attention to this issue.

In terms of health care, America's greatest public health crisis is the AIDS/HIV epidemic, but relatively few whites seem to recognize the unequal impact of AIDS within minority communities. In 1993, half of all American AIDS and HIV cases were African Americans and Latinos. As Yale law professor Harlon Dalton observes, within minority communities "there is a justifiable fear that public concern for the epidemic will wane...as soon as it becomes understood that the face of AIDS has darkened." Where has America seen this in the press?

The same parallel universe of race and class exists in American economics. The biggest "losers" in the recessions in the early 1990s, says the Economic Policy Institute, were African Americans. "An unprecedented number of the new jobs created in the recovery have been either temporary or part-time," its report concludes—employment in which minorities are often trapped.

Apparently, few of us—black or white—really want to discuss the root causes of America's parallel racial universes, where most whites experience economic growth, positive health care treatment and access to quality housing, and where minorities can expect just the opposite. The common denominator that links blacks' lost wages, poor health care, rural poverty and insurance discrimination is an endemic lack of power. Racism = prejudice + power. So long as African Americans and other racial minorities lack effective power—economic, social or governmental—we will consistently continue to be marginalized and oppressed.

How do we overcome such a legacy of inequality and the continuing burden of race? To deconstruct racial barriers, we all must actively foster an environment of multicultural dialogue and understanding. People cannot talk to each other if they are influenced by stereotypes and half-truths about other Americans who, though they live, shop, work and raise their children in the same communities, are "different" from themselves. Media, film and educational institutions have a decisive role to play in overturning America's pervasive images of inequality. Before we can realize Martin Luther King's dream of a society grounded in human equality and multicultural understanding, we still must find ways to promote accurate cultural and social images that illuminate the real problems experienced by people of color in contemporary America.

Manning Marable is a professor of history and political science and director of the Institute for Research in African-American Studies at Columbia University. His books include Race, Reform and Rebellion: The Second Reconstruction *(1991) and* The Crisis of Color and Democracy *(1992).*

II
Covering America

3

Immigration, the Press and the New Racism

John J. Miller

Whenever immigrants make the news these days, it seems it's always bad news. In May 1994, a federal judge handed down life sentences—280-year terms—to three Palestinians and an Egyptian convicted in New York's World Trade Center bombing. The previous March, New York police charged a Lebanese immigrant in the drive-by shooting of Hasidic Jewish students on the Brooklyn Bridge. In December 1993, a Jamaican immigrant killed six commuters and wounded 17 others in a rush-hour massacre on the Long Island Rail Road. Before that came the fiasco over Zoë Baird's immigrant nanny and the shipwreck off a New York City beach of the *Golden Venture,* which carried hundreds of illegal Chinese immigrants. Cued by popular sentiment, the governors of California, Florida, Texas and Arizona have sued the federal government for billions of dollars to recover costs those states spend on illegal immigrants. Even the lurid Bobbitt affair had an immigration twist—Lorena is from Ecuador.

Such stories drive down immigrants' acceptance among the public on Main Street, which has never been very high, even though nearly all of our families started as immigrants. Last summer, 60 percent of Americans told a *Newsweek* poll that immigrants are a "bad thing" for the country today. A *New York Times*/CBS News survey found that 61 percent would like to see a cut in current immigration levels, up from 49 percent who wanted curbs in 1986 when Congress passed the Immigration Reform and Control Act.

The media, of course, aren't responsible for this environment. Immigrants have always made Americans uneasy, and most of the traditional

21

complaints still make the rounds today: Immigrants cost more than they're worth, they ruin neighborhoods, they drain welfare, they steal jobs. None of these accusations carries much truth, but they easily (and frequently) make their way into newsprint and onto the airwaves, a constant part of our political landscape since the nation was founded. The media can't do anything about that. What the media *can* do, however, is exacerbate or ease these worries. It all comes down to the quality of reporting on immigrant issues.

One problem is the drive to give the masses what they want. It's little more than a marketing strategy. Here's how it works: If the public doesn't like immigrants, then let them know how *bad* they are, and don't let facts get in the way. I recently spoke with a television news producer on the West Coast who was assigned a story on how immigrants are supposedly clogging the U.S. prison system. After scratching beneath the surface of a few widely reported but dubious statistics, she uncovered a startling and inconvenient truth: Immigrants are no more prone to crime than the native population. But her bosses didn't want that story. They wanted red meat for the nativists. She went ahead and did the story as best she could, but wasn't entirely satisfied with the results.

A much bigger problem arises when reporters who don't know the basics of immigration policy and law have to venture into this unfamiliar territory. Not every news bureau has a reporter who covers immigration in much detail, but almost every community will at some point find its news affected by immigration. Sometimes reporters will make a mistake simply because they don't know any better. In summer 1993, *Newsweek* devoted one of its covers to an "Immigration Backlash." In a sidebar on "The Economic Cost of Immigration," it turned to Donald Huddle, whom it identified as an "immigration expert" at Rice University. It then reported Huddle's estimate that immigrants will cost taxpayers about $50 billion per year for the next decade. That's the difference between what they use in government services and what they pay in taxes, according to Huddle. It's also a huge number—about one-fifth of this year's federal budget deficit.

With a little bit more legwork, *Newsweek*'s reporters would have discovered that Huddle leaves a long paper trail of shoddy scholarship on the economics of immigration. No genuine "immigration expert" takes him seriously. What's more, Huddle didn't present his findings to scholars at an academic conference. He turned them over to his sponsors at the Carrying Capacity Network, a Washington-based wing of the zero population growth movement. (Immigrants contribute to as much as half of U.S. population growth, so the population control crowd opposes most immigration.) In other words, the agency that commissioned Huddle's research is a special interest group with an anti-immigrant axe to grind, which *Newsweek,* in turn, treated as a credible and dispassionate source of information. That's like relying on Fidel Castro for analysis of Cuba's economic vitality.

Few people now take Huddle's latest outburst seriously, however, thanks to the work of Jeffrey Passel and Rebecca Clark of the Urban Institute. They showed Huddle's research as more than just flawed. For example, Huddle assumes that revenue estimates from legal immigrants living in Los Angeles County who arrived during the 1980s are representative of *all* legal immigrants who entered the United States from 1970 to 1992, a blunder that leads him to take the $9,700 average per capita income of the L.A. County immigrants and apply it to legal immigrants nationwide. In so doing, he underestimates the per capita income of legal immigrants nationally by well over $4,000. These revisions were widely reported when they came out, and the *New York Times* op-ed page even featured a pro-con forum with Huddle and the Urban Institute team. But Huddle still sneaks into the news—the *Los Angeles Times, Orlando Sentinel, Sacramento Bee* and many other papers have recently referred to his work in a less-than-critical fashion. In most cases, this is not the work of immigration beat reporters. It comes from journalists in search of the flashiest figure available.

When immigrants get a bum rap, it's often because a writer reports the hard-luck story of a small group of people in a single place. A recent feature in the *Atlantic Monthly* by Roy Beck, for example, takes a close look at Wausau, Wis., and the many Laotian refugees who resettled there after fleeing their homeland. Beck calls attention to the inevitable culture clash that comes with putting Laotians in an almost entirely homogeneous white community. He lists the grievances of longtime residents, says that Laotians are crowding the schools and worries about the possibility of more Laotians arriving soon. Wausau, it turns out, has a few unique problems and challenges. So do most cities and towns. But by the time he wraps up his reporting, Beck has called for a moratorium on all immigration. The country needs to go through a period of "social healing," he concludes, in order "to achieve a unified and harmonious culture—the paradigm of a recoverable paradise" (whatever that may be). From his close look at a small group of refugees in the Midwest, Beck somehow manages to take away a rather broad set of lessons for the whole country and its many kinds of immigrants from many different places.

Beck isn't just sloppy, he's devious. Like Huddle, he comes to his task with an agenda. Beck works as Washington correspondent for *The Social Contract,* a deservedly obscure quarterly magazine with a distinct nativist flair. *Atlantic Monthly,* to its credit, listed Beck's affiliation. but most readers don't know anything about *The Social Contract.* They could wrongly think that they're getting a fair-minded appraisal from an unbiased journalist. What they're really getting is a hack who hates immigrants.

No matter what Beck would have us believe, there's really no such thing as an "immigrant." No single immigrant can stand in for the rest. Each varies enormously by country of origin, race, ethnicity, age, education and in countless other ways. Perhaps the most fundamental distinction centers on legal status: who is a legal immigrant, who is undocumented, and who is a refugee. When somebody lumps together these fundamentally different categories, bad information often winds up masquerading as the truth. On a whole range of issues, immigrants often get short-changed by reporters who don't know what they're talking about.

Take welfare. Everybody in Washington talks about welfare reform these days. Many in Congress have proposed welfare schemes that would cut aid to immigrants in order to pay for job training among citizens. Immigrants aren't eligible for most forms of welfare, but some of them can make use of certain varieties. The unspoken assumption is that immigrants are dragging down the whole welfare system. Careful examination suggests otherwise.

It's true that immigrants are more likely to receive welfare than natives. But it's only part of the story. Problem is, refugees use welfare at the high rate of 15.6 percent, according to the Urban Institute's recent analysis of 1990 Census data. Refugees account for about one out of seven legal immigrants. That's not a lot, but it skews the welfare numbers. Among nonrefugee immigrants, welfare use comes in at 4.1 percent. Native Americans, it turns out, use welfare at a 4.2 percent rate. Among working-age people, the gap widens. What's more, welfare use among all immigrants actually declined during the 1980s, a period that many immigration restrictionists have criticized for the admission of unskilled immigrants.

Refugees, of course, are a special case. Most of them flee from their homes not because of any grand plan to immigrate, but out of sheer need. Refugee policy is humanitarian policy—its immediate goals have little to do with family reunification or economic self-interest, the guiding principles of all other immigration. The United States admits refugees because, without the help of foreign governments, they would be left to suffer the ravages of war and persecution in Bosnia, Iraq, Rwanda and elsewhere. The government then provides special assistance available only to refugees, since the personal and economic traumas of being forcibly uprooted and resettled in a strange new land make a powerful case for help. If the United States refused to provide this emergency aid—or provided temporary low-interest guaranteed loans instead of handouts, for example—then refugee welfare rates would be just as low as other immigrant groups. As things stand, refugees do climb the ladder to success in America. It just takes them a bit longer.

Subtleties like these make all the difference in immigration reporting, but writers like Roy Beck would just as soon ignore them.

If it's not welfare, then it's jobs. Immigrants have traditionally had to fight the notion that they take jobs away from the native-born. Over the last several months, editorials in the *Dallas Morning News, Houston Chronicle* and *Phoenix Gazette* have all made this point. So have some business publications, like the *Journal of Commercial Lending*. The *National Review* recently cheered a bill that would tie levels of legal immigration to the unemployment rate.

But again, studies from the academic world are fairly consistent in denying these charges. Earlier this year, the Alexis de Tocqueville Institute released a report from economists Richard Vedder and Lowell Gallaway of Ohio University and Stephen Moore of the Cato Institute. It identified the 10 states with the highest average percentage of immigrants from 1960 to 1990 and compared them with the 10 states with the smallest relative immigrant presence. In the first group, median unemployment during the period was 5.9 percent. For the second group, it was 6.6 percent. The study also found a higher proportion of immigrants in the 10 states with the lowest rate of joblessness during the 1980s than in the 10 states with the worst unemployment problems. As the authors wrote in their summary, "more immigrants, less unemployment."

Many critics say that although immigrants may serve society as a whole, they compete mainly with low-skilled natives, especially blacks. Thomas Muller looked at this question in his recent book, *Immigrants and the American City*. He used 1989 data in reporting lower unemployment for both black men and black women in areas with large amounts of immigration from Mexico. Muller's work yielded similar results for areas experiencing heavy Korean immigration. These findings could mean that Mexicans and Koreans settle in areas that offer good employment opportunities for everybody, including blacks. Or they could mean that these immigrants actually create jobs for blacks. In either case, they strongly suggest that the presence of immigrants does not directly cause joblessness among blacks.

Other data indicate that black household incomes rise in areas with a high-percentage of foreign-born residents, that immigration levels do very little to explain unemployment among black youths, and that middle-class blacks living in "gateway cities" with many immigrants made significant strides during the 1980s toward reducing black-white income differentials. Immigration does not present a rosy scenario for all blacks, of course. Immigrant labor often undercuts trade union contracts. Some evidence suggests that in a shrinking economy, immigrants will slightly depress wage levels for low-skilled workers. Illegal immigrants, incidentally, do not hurt the labor market opportunities of natives either. According to the small amount of evidence available, they may actually increase employment and wages. The only group of people that clearly suffers from newly arrived immigrants are other recent immigrants, since they often wind up competing for the same kinds of employment.

The most common stereotype surrounding immigrants—more common than welfare and job worries—is that immigration policy is somehow "out of control." Who hasn't seen some television crew film a herd of poor Mexicans swiftly weaving their way through the borderline traffic jams near San Diego? It's a grim sight, and it feeds popular misperceptions. According to the *New York Times*/CBS News poll, 68 percent of the public thinks that most recent immigrants are illegal. The government just can't seem to get its act together on the border, says the conventional wisdom.

Fact is, today's immigration policy has been carefully reasoned and debated. It may not be the best policy imaginable, or one that satisfies everybody, but it came into being through democratic deliberation. In absolute terms, the current influx is roughly as large as the one that arrived in the early part of the century. About 800,000 immigrants enter legally each year. As many as 300,000 illegal immigrants also settle permanently. Less than half of this latter group comes from Mexico.

The intellectual case supporting high levels of immigration to the United States (let alone the historic precedents) is so overwhelmingly one-sided that it's surprising to find anyone who opposes it. But sometimes when heads pull in one direction, hearts tug in another. What may worry people most is this: The new immigrants look different. Some fear the "browning" of America, since so many of the latest wave of huddled masses, yearning to be free, come from Asia, the Caribbean and Latin America instead of from Europe. Think back on the enduring Haitian stalemate: What if Haitians weren't black? Would that change the whole political equation? Would Presidents Bush and Clinton have been more prone to absorb those newcomers, as similar newcomers are welcomed as escapees and refugees from the post-Cold War artifact of Cuba?

From 1951 to 1960, only 2.5 million mostly European immigrants made their way to our shores. Germany served as the largest feeder nation, the source of over 477,000 newcomers. Next came Canada, with just under 378,000. Today, Europeans account for less than one-fifth of the total. Mexicans led the way among legal immigrants in 1992, followed by Vietnamese, Filipinos, former Soviets and Dominicans. More Pakistanis made the trip than Germans, more Taiwanese than Canadians. Since more than two-thirds of all immigrants settle in just four states—California (38 percent), New York (14 percent), Florida (8 percent) and Texas (8 percent)—their populations are highly concentrated and visible.

This factor may underlie the whole debate. The common accusations about high costs, neighborhood decline, welfare use and job competition serve as covers for closet xenophobes who won't admit in public that they are uncomfortable with the racial and ethnic makeup of today's immigrants. That these complaints don't have much empirical support makes their case a tough sell, but sloppy journalism turns a complex and encouraging reality into a simplistic and ominous fiction. We owe it to the immigrants—and ourselves—to set matters straight.

John J. Miller is associate director of the Manhattan Institute's Center for the New American Community in Washington, D.C.

4

African Americans According to TV News

Robert M. Entman

While journalists strive to portray the news objectively (or at least fairly), it is no secret that constructing the news requires subjective judgments. Limited in resources and time, under great competitive pressure, TV news organizations in particular must select, simplify and organize the day's events into a meaningful and visually compelling narrative.

My research suggests a disturbing by-product of television's news-making processes. The choices TV journalists make appear to feed racial stereotypes, encouraging white hostility and fear of African Americans. TV news, especially local news, paints a picture of blacks as violent and threatening toward whites, self-interested and demanding toward the body politic—continually causing problems for the law-abiding, tax-paying majority.

We have all heard that sensationalism and entertainment values are on the rise in TV news. My studies indicate these trends aren't simply professional embarrassments and frustrations for journalists. They may also be making urban America less governable, deepening the chasm of misunderstanding and distrust between blacks and whites.

Scholars believe that people process information by using stored categories called schemas. Schemas are like mental filing cabinets that allow the individual to group like objects together in the mind. By assimilating new data with what's already stored in a schema, individuals interpret and make sense of the bits and pieces of new information they encounter.

But this mental organizational system can create the inaccurate beliefs and negative emotions that underpin prejudiced thinking: stereotypes. If the new information an individual keeps encountering fits the negative categories, prejudiced thinking can develop and grow.

Despite considerable progress, white Americans still exhibit a high degree of racial prejudice. For example, in the 1992 National Election Study (the authoritative academic public opinion survey from the University of Michigan), 57.4 percent of white respondents rated blacks as lazier than whites; 66 percent of whites rated blacks as more violence-prone; 49.4 percent of whites said blacks were less intelligent. Since there is a demonstrated tendency for whites to misrepresent their true racial feelings (it is socially undesirable to express overt anti-black bigotry to strangers such as survey interviewers), these data probably understate the degree of racial stereotyping. It seems reasonable to assume at least half the white audience is bigoted and susceptible to having their negative stereotypes confirmed, deepened and activated by TV news.

A series of scholarly studies on images of blacks in TV news that I have conducted suggests that newsroom procedures and definitions of news combine with selected aspects of the real world to encourage negative stereotypes about blacks. My research focuses mainly on local Chicago news, but other work indicates similar patterns elsewhere, including that of Erna Smith at San Francisco State University on coverage of the Los Angeles riots, and Kathleen Hall Jamieson at the University of Pennsylvania on local news in several urban markets. Network news differs as a genre from typical local newscasts, but some images of African Americans presented by the networks appear equally problematic. The damage comes especially from reporting on crime and violence, politics and poverty.

Research reveals that for the three dominant network affiliates in Chicago, eight or nine minutes out of about 14 given to news on an average half-hour broadcast in late 1993 and early 1994 concerned the threat of violence to humans. A steady drumbeat of frightening information dominates local news. And there's a racial skew to this scary stuff. For example, black defendants were more likely to be shown in still photos or mug shots, with no name appearing on the screen. White defendants, on the other hand, were more frequently named, and were represented through a variety of visual images, particularly, still photos and motion video. Such subtle visual differences may contribute to white perceptions of blacks as an undifferentiated group, while whites, named and portrayed in more detail, retain individual identities.

At the same time, blacks are significantly more likely to appear in the physical custody of police officials than are whites. The symbolic message is that, even when accused of similar crimes, blacks are more dangerous than whites. A negative and emotional stereotype may be unconsciously reinforced by whites' year-in, year-out exposure to this pattern of images.

The basic scholarly understanding of prejudiced thinking is that people from the dominant "in group" (whites) perceive members of the disliked "outgroup" (blacks) as homogeneous, and blanket them with negative associations. The key element of anti-black racism is whites' tendency to lump all or most blacks together as possessing undesirable traits.

Finally, the research showed that local TV news was far more likely to depict whites than minorities in an official law enforcement capacity, or in unofficial "helper" or "good Samaritan" roles. In my latest research, about 12 white law enforcers were shown for every black one, a ratio that underrepresents the true proportion of blacks in metropolitan Chicago police departments. As for helpers, the local news sample included 450 minutes devoted to showing white samaritans, 33 minutes to stories depicting black samaritans. The overall image of crime and violence from local news is one in which minorities, especially blacks, play a heavy role in causing violence but contribute disproportionately little toward helping society cope with it.

Additional analysis probed the image of blacks in political news, and findings were no more positive. Direct quotes (sound bites) from black activists, politicians or officials made them appear much more selfish and demanding than their white counterparts. In one study, some 33 percent of all assertions made by blacks endorsing or criticizing a government policy demanded attention to the black community. Whites explicitly promoted their ethnic group interests only 5 percent of the time. Indeed, white leaders were shown more often explicitly defending black political interests than openly advancing their own group's self-interests.

This image of black politics is not wholly a creation of journalists. It reflects real characteristics of the political system. Having been shut out of the power structure for so long, African-American leaders may indeed speak up largely for black interests. But it is highly unlikely that white political actors are as purely civic-minded as they appear. Since white politicians already dominate, they do not have to use an overt rhetoric of white power. To protect the status quo and their group's position in it, they need only speak of the public interest or nonracial values such as meritocracy or low taxes.

In theory, the depictions of black demands could be offering a powerful platform for African Americans. But academic theories of modern American racism suggest a boomerang effect: White audiences may infer that blacks seek a lot from government, receive quite a bit of support from whites, but fail to return the favor by supporting policy beneficial to whites. Moreover, the presentation of black spokespersons often includes snippets of loud, angry or emotional rhetoric: The televisual sound bite predominates over the calm analysis and justification of the black community's legitimate grievances.

Negative images of blacks in politics are not restricted to local TV news. In one year of network news coverage, more than one-third of the stories mentioning black leaders included an accusation that the leader committed a crime. Here again, the news reflects some aspects of reality—there are few blacks in top federal leadership positions that are automatically newsworthy. Thus, black leaders receive prolonged media attention only when they are involved in some kind of crime or controversy. The result is a comparatively more positive picture of white leadership in network news.

Consider reporting on Washington Mayor Marion Barry. In the year sampled, Barry was the second most commonly mentioned black figure (Clarence Thomas was number one). The coverage of Barry's drug arrest accurately reflected the experience of a scurrilous politician who happened to be black. But there are hundreds of effective, conscientious black mayors toiling around the United States who together attained only a fraction of the network visibility accorded Barry. That the Barry stories comprised a high proportion of network images of black politicians is due to news standards that emphasize unusual controversy and drama— to the extraordinary videotape showing Barry committing apparent crimes—not to a reality that the typical black mayor uses drugs and consorts with shady characters. Nonetheless, given how prejudiced people process information, we can predict that the accurate but frequent and sensational reports of Barry's crimes, arrest and conviction promoted inaccurate stereotypes among many whites.

Beyond its active contribution to stereotyping, TV news may be having deleterious effects on black-white relations through omission and indirection in covering poverty. Television news seldom addresses poverty and its causes explicitly. Rather, TV makes implicit arguments about poverty by showing images of its symptoms. For example, stories on violent crime, drug abuse and gangs contain visual images of urban blight and stereotyped references to geographic locations that provide implicit links to poverty. One story included in the research portrayed the murder of a little girl, allegedly by her mother. Viewers learned the crime was committed in an "abandoned building" in a "drug-infested neighborhood" by somebody with a history of mental illness. The report associated one poverty symptom—violent crime—with others—drug abuse, mental illness—and visually linked them to poverty by showing pictures of blighted buildings and identifying the neighborhood as Chicago's South Side, widely known for its high concentration of poor residents.

The visual and verbal images of poverty symptoms suggest poverty is overwhelmingly concentrated among blacks, so much so that merely showing black persons appears to be a TV code for the involvement of poor people in the news event. The connection between "black" and "poor" exists even though poverty is not the lot of most black persons, and more whites are poor than black. The concepts of "black person" and "poverty" are so thoroughly intertwined in television news that the white public's perceptions of poverty appear difficult to disentangle from their thinking about African Americans. (A national survey by Mark Peffley of the University of Kentucky and his colleagues supports this notion.) That connection promotes a stereotyped and inaccurate understanding of the economic and social diversity of the African-American community, a misapprehension that itself could feed bigotry and lower support among whites for public policy that tackles poverty.

Because television news offers only implicit information about the relationship between poverty, race and crime, viewers are left with no coherent explanation of poverty issues. Only indirectly does TV news suggest, for example, that racial discrimination might have something to do with poverty, which in turn may help explain all that crime. Beyond the common visual links, there is little in the news to draw poverty symptoms together as interrelated causes and consequences that are not merely the individual doing of the poor. Even the nonracist white audience receives few messages that might allow them to reconcile their legitimate self-interest in low taxes and personal safety with what might be called their moral self-interest, their desire to alleviate the human suffering of the poor.

But the inattention to poverty as a policy problem is hardly TV's fault alone. Television news is locked in a self-reinforcing political climate with politicians who see few votes to be gained in speaking sympathetically about the poor. The lack of serious political rhetoric about poverty causes a dearth in TV coverage of poverty as a policy issue—the public fails to see poverty as a pressing matter—and that discourages politicians still more from targeting poverty.

Determining whether this pattern of images and gaps actually affects audiences is a difficult proposition, but scientific surveys designed to measure racist attitudes suggest a connection between exposure to television news and the extent of anti-black racism in the public. While these findings are far from definitive, they do indicate that the images of blacks in the news contribute to the perpetuation of anti-black stereotypes. A survey of Chicago-area residents found that whites who rely on television for their news were more likely than those who rely on print or radio to deny that blacks are discriminated against. Similarly, heavy television viewers were more likely than light viewers to stereotype blacks as being unskilled and lazy. (This analysis controlled for education and other demographic traits.)

The absence of a visual dimension to radio news and the infrequent use of photographs in print stories involving blacks means that for these media, the race of individuals in stories is seldom known. But television's visuals tend to make race an explicit part of the news text. A lack of much exposure to print news may prevent opportunities to have stereotypes challenged. At the same time, those with less racial sympathy may be more willing to put up with the unflattering images of blacks that permeate TV news.

Racial stereotypes in the news pose a difficult problem for television journalists. Reporters do not construct messages from scratch. The images that dominate local and network TV news are grounded in elements of reality. Young black males are statistically more likely to commit violent crime than young white males; black leaders may more often express demands for government services than white leaders whose constituents are on average better off; most American cities do have poverty-ridden black neighborhoods. Therefore, one could argue, the news merely reflects unfortunate reality. But for the media to achieve a comprehensive accuracy in portraying any reality is impossible. The news can offer only partial, selective representations. While individual stories about blacks may accurately reflect a particular slice of reality, they may over time construct a distorted impression in the minds of white (and black) audience members.

And this is the crux of the problem TV journalists face: Is their responsibility limited to creating an accurate verbal and visual record in each individual news text, or does it include stimulating an accurate mental representation in the audience's mind? Presumably helping the audience understand truth is what justifies professional news standards and practices. Textual accuracy for its own sake seems an unlikely candidate for journalism's ultimate goal.

Television news is uniquely poised to reduce racial stereotyping. But to do so, TV journalists must realize that their words and images, however accurate on a story-by-story basis, accumulate over time to exacerbate racial tensions. A deliberate choice to introduce more complexity and variety in images of African Americans could, on balance, make TV news less likely to arouse white antagonism rooted in misunderstanding and stereotype—while offering a more comprehensively accurate depiction of African-American life.

Innovations in news could include an increase in serious reporting on policy issues which, unlike single violent episodes that directly affect only a few people, speak to almost everyone in the audience. This is not to gainsay the importance of reporting on violence, or to minimize the suffering it causes. But mere cataloging of the day's unfortunate victims, uncontrollable disasters, and scary criminals appears to inflame more than inform the public. Other changes might include less frequently revealing the ethnicity of accused perpetrators through pictures; minimizing the use of frightening images (wounded people on stretchers, flashing lights of police cars, flames); and reordering priorities so that news of individual violent incidents receive less news time and prominence.

We must acknowledge, however, that actions taken to ameliorate one false impression could heighten another. For example, reducing images of black crime and victimization could instill among whites an unwarranted sense of progress in the inner city. Similarly, deliberate use of successful black experts as sources, while perhaps counterbalancing all the criminals and victims, could simultaneously feed the complacency of whites who insist racial discrimination has ceased. And correcting the implication that blacks are more demanding of government responsiveness than whites could lead to airtime for safe, white-anointed black leaders who enjoy slim legitimacy in the African-American community.

While there is no easy way out of such dilemmas, they point to the familiar need for context. By routinely contextualizing, TV news could reveal the continued prevalence of discrimination, illuminate structural forces that make crime attractive in the ghetto, and explain why so many black political leaders adopt a confrontational style. But complex, nuanced context is difficult for daily TV news to convey. Perhaps the first step toward improving accuracy and social responsibility in the portrayal of blacks on television news is acknowledging these difficulties.

Robert M. Entman is an associate professor of communication studies at Northwestern University, and was a visiting professor at North Carolina State University in 1994–95. He gratefully acknowledges the support of the Chicago Community Trust Human Relations Foundation and the assistance of James B. White in preparing this article.

5

From Bad to Worse—The Media's Framing of Race and Risk

Oscar H. Gandy Jr.

Although we may have taken it as fact that bad news sells—and that bad news with pictures sells even better—many of us have begun to question whether all this selling produces benefits without cost. Increasingly, we have come to question whether the news media's revealed preference for the negative has consequences for the national spirit. To the extent that the mass media have made us see the world as a mean and dangerous place, they have diminished the quality of our lives. And, to the extent that they have emphasized the ways in which the distribution of social and economic risks breaks down along racial lines, they have helped to tear us apart.

Of course, reporters and editors do not set out to make us fear, mistrust, resent or pity each other. These consequences are what economists refer to as "externalities," spillover effects that arise from the use of a particular technology. We readily understand that air pollution is the unintended result of the use of particular fuels. We should understand that cultural pollution occurs in a very similar way. Advertisements that use scantily clad women to attract the attention of male consumers contribute to the degradation of the image of women in the society. In similar fashion, the use of headlines, statistics and graphic examples to attract the attention of politically involved white readers to an investigative report on racial discrimination, for example, contributes to the definition of African Americans as hapless victims at the same time that it leads blacks to overestimate the risks and oppression they actually face.

Journalistic traditions that are taught in the classroom and reinforced in editorial conferences represent a technology that produces a distorted impression of the world. The reduction in the number of competing newspapers in the nation's urban markets means that the greatest variation in the use of these techniques may be found between, rather than within, cities. The fact that these impressions may also vary systematically with the race and ethnic identity of the readership further complicates the task of adjusting this technology so as to reduce its harmful effects.

We do well to doubt that our impressions of the world around us are fully determined by media coverage, yet the evidence of media influence is quite strong. Of course, our understanding of the world outside our immediate personal experience is influenced by a number of sources—including close friends, colleagues and acquaintances—but the media's influence is more substantial than we may recognize. The work of media scholar George Gerbner and his colleagues has led a virtual army of researchers to demonstrate over and over again that the amount of time an individual spends watching television predicts a tendency to describe the world in the same distorted way as it has been presented on the tube in news and fiction.

The logic of this so-called cultivation model is hard to fault. Because the television image carries the impression of realism, even the clearly fictional representations of prime-time serials provide the raw material from which we construct our own pictures of the world. Thus, the more time we spend in the world of television, the more we understand the world in television terms. Because violence plays such a critical role in storytelling, it seems obvious that people who watch more television will observe more acts of violence and will thereby be influenced to see the world as a more violent and dangerous place than it really is.

Because of the media's role in the cultivation of social perceptions, there is reason to be concerned about the tendency for African Americans and Hispanics to be presented in media roles that define them as violent criminals. Not only do such representations operate to reproduce racism, but the cumulative impact of such coverage may be a reduction in the general audience's willingness to support public policies designed to help blacks escape poverty and criminal victimization. This reluctance is based on a well-founded sense that blacks are criminals, and criminals don't need help—they need to be punished!

Shanto Iyengar, in his important book *Is Anybody Responsible?*, demonstrates that traditions in journalism that favor episodic over thematic frames for stories lead the public toward assigning blame and responsibility to individuals rather than to organizations or institutions. Where individuals are understood to be responsible for their own misfortune, there is no place for a public response beyond punishment.

My own work has begun to question just what the social consequences might be of changes in the nature of journalistic practice that may result in an increase in the number of stories reporting on the social risks that are faced by African Americans. Although investigative journalism continues its traditional mission of identifying villains and victims, the use of the computer has increased the number of stories that present the evidence of wrongdoing in statistical terms. On one hand, the increase in such databased stories almost guarantees that thematic frames will be used, even if individual cases of suffering may be inserted into the story to illustrate the nature of the problem in human-interest terms. According to theory, such a framing ought to produce a greater sense of institutional responsibility. On the other hand, statistical evidence of risk is frequently presented in ways that distort the facts and lead to the expression of preferences that are hard to justify on a purely rational basis.

By examining how stories about the social risks that African Americans face are framed, we might begin to understand why citizens of different races have come to think of themselves and others in the ways that they do. We might also learn something about the reasons for their support or opposition to particular social policies and the governments that propose them.

Each of us faces some degree of risk when we enter the market for goods and services. The current love affair Americans seem to have with the marketplace as a guarantor of all sorts of values beyond allocative efficiency assumes that this market provides value in exchange for its equivalent. This is an assumption of equality. The finding that differences in the values actually received are linked to differences in the race of the consumer raises concern about the operation of the market. An observed disparity may be newsworthy in itself; that the disparity is the product of illegal racial discrimination is quite a different story, one that has implications for public trust, and that calls for a policy response.

The difference between a story about discrimination and a story about disparity is one of subtle framing. That these differences in framing might be explained by reference to the structural characteristics of a newspaper's market or the racial composition of its editorial staff raises troubling questions about the nature of press performance.

As part of my project as a fellow at The Freedom Forum Media Studies Center, I examined the ways in which stories about racial disparity—or differential risk—were framed in the nation's leading newspapers. Several different strategies were used to uncover patterns of editorial framing. By searching a computerized database for stories that used the word *black* within 10 words of the words *more likely* or *less likely*, we were able to select a sample of phrases that made use of what I refer to as the actuarial assumption—that statistical data gathered in the past could be useful for predicting what would occur in the future. For example, "Blacks are far less likely than whites to receive a mortgage" was a commonly used comparative phrase. This strategy identified a large number of phrases that compared the risks faced by whites and blacks that we classified into four primary types: high probability of black loss, low probability of black success, high probability of white success, or low probability of white loss. Even though the underlying story captured by these phrases concerned disparities in which whites usually got more than blacks, we were nevertheless surprised to find that out of 411 such phrases, nearly 75 percent were framed in terms of the high probability of black loss, not the high probability of white success.

Because of an interest in the treatment of institutionalized racism, where the risks that African Americans face in society can be identified with the decisions made by officials, experts or bureaucrats, we examined a smaller sample of stories that fell into six categories of risk: 1) economic risks, as in those stories reporting racial disparity in the granting of mortgages; 2) health risks, as in those stories reporting racial disparity in the use of bypass surgery; 3) education, as in those stories about racial disparity in tracking or in the assignment of students to ability groups; 4) government services, as in those stories about racial disparity in the determination of eligibility for disability benefits; 5) criminal justice, as in those stories about racial disparity in convictions and sentences; and 6) employment, as in those stories about racial disparity in hiring, promotion or dismissal.

For these stories, differences in framing were sought in the headlines and the lead paragraphs. We examined the stories to determine whether they were framed in terms of disparity, bias or discrimination, as well as the degree to which the headlines and leads emphasized the high probability of black loss or the low probability of black success. Again, the stories' tendency was to favor the high probability of black loss over other options for framing the story.

We also identified four national stories that were sufficiently newsworthy to have been carried by the majority of the national papers in our database, facilitating an electronic search. Increasing the number of papers examined made it possible to explore some characteristics of the markets as factors that might explain similarities and differences in the framing of these stories.

The stories we examined through the "Papers" file of the Dialog database were those having to do with disparities in the granting of disability payments, differences in the use of bypass surgery and differences in the granting of mortgages. Of the four major stories we examined, only in the 1993 story about disparities in medical treatment did we find many departures from the tendency toward emphasizing black loss. For this story, nearly 40 percent of the headlines emphasized white patients' success in receiving aggressive medical treatment. This compares with 62 percent of the headlines that emphasized denial of such treatment to blacks in a similar story in 1992, and 65 percent of the headlines emphasizing denial of disability benefits to blacks.

We also examined patterns in story framing in different papers as a function of the size of the African-American population in the newspaper's metropolitan area, and as a function of the number of minority group members who were on the paper's editorial staff. Because the most stories were about disparity in mortgage lending, this story had the greatest potential to reveal the role of these kinds of structural influences on differences in story framing. First, we noted that this story was more likely to be framed in terms of bias or discrimination than were any of the other stories. This tendency was even stronger in those markets where African Americans represented a larger share of the potential readership. The data suggest that some papers were less likely to frame the stories as questioning the evidence or the conclusions in those studies. Indeed, the fewer blacks there were in the market, the *more* likely these stories were to be framed in terms of uncertainty and doubt.

Because editorial decisions are made with a primary readership in mind, we can understand how content and framing may differ between markets when the racial composition differs substantially. Although editors resist the suggestion that the influence of advertiser preference for an upscale white audience may be reflected in content, alternative explanations are no more comforting. Urban planners are well aware of the existence of a "tipping point" beyond which white flight accelerates and the racial composition of neighborhoods and schools begins to change dramatically. Editors may be responding to a similar sense of changes in their audience, and they may change their content either to hold on to their white readers or to attract a larger share of black readers within their market. This kind of strategic move will have unintended consequences for understanding, preferences and choices within that community that go far beyond the newspaper's bottom line.

At the same time, changes in the composition of the newsroom's professional staff may introduce new pressures on editorial decision-making. Minority staff, especially when their presence reaches a critical mass where they may respond as a group, may challenge the selection and framing of stories about race in ways that conflict with market-oriented strategies suggested by a newspaper's consultants. Using data from the annual report on minority newsroom presence from the American Society of Newspaper Editors, we added minority staff presence as another factor that might explain patterns in story framing.

The influence of minority staff is substantial. However, in several comparisons, we found that the presence of minorities on the staff seems to pull the papers in one direction, while the presence of minorities in the market tends to pull the papers in the other. For example, while greater black presence in the market is associated with a tendency to frame stories in terms of bias or discrimination, papers are *less* likely to frame their stories in this way if they have very many minorities on staff. These differences were quite substantial, despite the fact that there was a tendency for markets with a greater black presence also to have more minorities on the editorial staff.

When we used regression analysis to examine the simultaneous influence of three variables measuring community wealth, black population and minority presence on staff, however, we found that the proportion of African Americans in the marketplace emerged as the most powerful of the three explanatory factors. If we understand this influence to be a manifestation of economic interests that reflect tensions between a newspaper's reliance on circulation vs. advertising revenue, then these data raise critical questions about the nature of editorial judgments. Ed Baker, in his recent book, *Advertising and a Democratic Press,* is particularly instructive in this regard. In his view, a democratic press ought to respond to reader interests more than to the interests and concerns of advertisers. He suggests that taxes might actually be used as a policy instrument to increase the influence of circulation on editorial decision-making. However, where interests may be seen to vary with the race and ethnic identification of the readership, reducing the influence of advertisers does not eliminate the consequences that flow from framing stories with one segment of the readership as the primary target of the communication.

If we grant that the framing of stories influences what we understand about the world in which we live, including how we understand and respond to the risks we may encounter there, then it is important to understand how the press tends to frame these stories. The data in this and related studies are surprisingly consistent in suggesting that the press prefers to present differences between the fortunes of whites and blacks in terms of the high probability of black loss—bad news for and about blacks. The same facts might be framed in four different ways, but the negative seems to be preferred. This is evidence of an editorial bias that, taken in the context of cultivation theory that indicates that people tend to see the world in ways that are framed in media accounts, has consequences for the cultivation of social perceptions about risks faced by blacks.

The potential social outcomes are complex and contradictory, especially in the context of markets served by only a single newspaper. For example, this framing may have consequences for black readers in terms of their overestimating the riskiness of their environment, and may lead them to choose what are, in fact, even riskier options. A different impression may be gained by whites whose own assessment of personal risk will be suppressed, as it is compared with the fate of blacks. Differences in estimation of the magnitude of the disparity and in the extent to which these differences are seen as an intolerable injustice may be reflected in differences in the confidence that whites and blacks have in community institutions.

Surveys indicate quite substantial differences between whites and blacks in terms of their belief in the existence of a broad-based conspiracy that produces greater hardship for blacks. Trust in institutions, respect for the law and participation in the political process are all shaped and reinforced by our constructions of social reality. The framing of stories about differential risk can not help but add to these impressions. The fact that differences in the framing of comparative risk vary with the characteristics of the markets in which newspapers are published raises critical questions about how well the press is performing its democratic function.

The story of risk does not have to be framed in comparative terms. Indeed, comparison ought not be the basis for determining a socially acceptable level of risk. But discrimination is itself a risk that must be covered if it is to be addressed as a social problem. The fact that the courts tend to assess discrimination in terms of disparate outcome as well as disparate treatment suggests that reliance on comparisons is a "second best" solution when a crime of great social violence rarely leaves a smoking gun.

I am not prepared to say that increasing the presence of minority news-room staff will produce the "right" framing for stories of differential risk. If it is clear that the same facts about risk can be presented in four different ways, and if it is also clear that our understanding of those risks varies with the ways in which the story is framed, depending upon who we are and with whom we identify, then there is no "right" frame. The best framing is one that produces relative equality or balance between types across similar stories. This implies that managing editors will have to take stock periodically and assess the ways in which stories about comparative risk are being framed. Editors know how to move toward balance.

Oscar H. Gandy Jr. is professor of communication at the Annenberg School for Communication at the University of Pennsylvania.

6

Covering the Invisible "Model Minority"

William Wong

Not all that long ago, Asian Americans could rightly complain that mainstream news media either ignored them or covered them in shallow, stereotypical ways.

In the 1970s, for instance, Asian gang stories were popular news items, spurred by spectacular real-life incidents like the 1977 Labor Day weekend massacre at the Golden Dragon restaurant in San Francisco (they remain a journalistic staple). In the 1980s, Asian Americans as the "model minority" was a theme of many stories, the emergence of a new stereotype.

Television coverage of Asian Americans remains spotty and sensationalized, but print coverage, while retaining some of the polar good-bad images, has become increasingly nuanced, textured and true to life, thanks in part to greater numbers of Asian American journalists, some of whom are bringing more informed coverage.

Their work, and that of enlightened non-Asian writers, shows up in a random sampling of stories over the past year or two:

- The Sunday, Sept. 26, 1993, *New York Times* Arts & Leisure section featured a piece by James R. Oestreich about the Ying siblings, a Chinese American classical string quartet that spent two years in Jesup, Iowa, on a cultural-arts education mission.
- Stephen Magagnini explained, in the Dec. 12, 1993, *Sacramento Bee,* how Southeast Asians were beginning to participate in American politics.
- Dwight Chapin, in the Feb. 15, 1994, *San Francisco Examiner,* profiled Helen Lum, a pioneering Chinese American tennis player.
- Jeanne Wong discussed in depth Sacramento's Korean American community in the May 23, 1993, *Sacramento Bee.*

• The *New York Times,* on Jan. 19, 1994, ran a feature about Kyong Sun Lee, a Korean American from Flushing, N.Y., who had quietly become the new world champion in the arcane sport of three-cushion billiards. The *Times* called him "the first American to win (the title) in 40 years." Not Korean American.

One example of how an Asian American journalist can make a difference is Himanee Gupta's cover article in the *Seattle Times' Pacific Magazine,* Dec. 12, 1993, "Seattle Masala: Balancing Indian Culture and the American Way of Life." Without pandering to stereotypes and broad generalizations, it was a nicely rendered piece about how young Indian Americans straddle two cultures.

American journalism has advanced by quantum leaps from the days when it was an active anti-Asian influence in this country, as there was in the 1870s, when newspapers drummed a hostile tune against Chinese laborers. This attitude helped create a political atmosphere that resulted in the 1882 Chinese Exclusion Act, which barred Chinese workers from the United States.

The American press helped shape public opinion against Japanese Americans during World War II that permitted more than 100,000 ethnic Japanese living on the West Coast, most of them U.S. citizens, to be hauled away into internment camps, without due process.

Journalism should, and frequently does, catch up with trends, and the Asian American growth pattern has been a story begging to be told in its many facets.

The biggest reason for improved coverage is the growth and complexity of the Asian American population itself. The U.S. Asian American population of 8 million has tripled since 1970, most noticeably in California, New York, Florida, Texas and Illinois, but also in areas that had few or no Asians before.

Broadly speaking, there are two Asian Americas—the old and the new. The "old" has its roots in the mid-19th century, when Chinese from Kwangtung province near Hong Kong first came in large numbers to mine gold, build America's transcontinental railroad and develop California's verdant agricultural lands. The Chinese were followed by Japanese and Filipinos. All suffered from institutionalized discrimination.

The "new" Asian America dates from 1965, when federal immigration laws were liberalized. The end of U.S. involvement in Vietnam in 1975 precipitated a continuing wave of refugees, which added to the growing migration of Asian immigrants. The result is a much more diverse Asian American population.

This diversity complicates the task of covering Asian America today. The many different Asian ethnic groups speak different languages, have different traditions, customs, histories and American experiences. Many want a piece of the American Dream; others come not out of hope but fear, in search of a safe haven.

Distinguishing between and among the various groups is important. The umbrella label of Asian Americans can be a useful, shorthand tool to politically identify the diverse Asian ethnic groups, and some Asian Americans embrace the label as a mark of political empowerment. Using "Asian American" is appropriate in the context of a couple of linked issues falling under the general category of discrimination or bias. Individuals belonging to different Asian ethnic groups sometimes experience subtle institutional discrimination known as the "glass ceiling." Sometimes they are targeted for bigoted attacks, or are mistaken for one another, in terms of ethnic identities. The idea of "foreignness" hangs over all Asian Americans, whether fifth-generation Americans or newly arrived refugees.

Therefore, whenever possible, precision in identifying Asian ethnic people in America and understanding who they are, are steps toward better journalism.

Other proven journalistic principles apply when covering the burgeoning Asian American story: good reporting, precise writing, cultivation of credible sources, knowledge of cultural traditions, histories and experiences. The assumption here is that journalism values the latter attributes, but shrinking newsroom resources and a tendency toward "tabloidization" steal from a newsroom the wherewithal to devote reporting time to study complex communities like Asian ethnic groups.

Progress hasn't eliminated some stubborn problems in covering Asian Americans, such as use of stereotypes and clichés and a general lack of knowledge. A continuing hole is an institutionalized national Asian American voice or voices of political and social commentaries. Varied African-American voices are heard in syndicated columns; even a few Latino columnists are beginning to emerge. Regular Asian American viewpoints are inaudible.

Some good reporting took place in one of the biggest stories in recent years involving an Asian ethnic group, the dramatic increase in the smuggling of Chinese nationals into the United States. Major news outlets in

New York and California gave that story a lot of attention in 1993 after a ship carrying almost 300 Chinese illegal immigrants in shocking conditions ran aground in New York waters.

A number of news organizations covered this story thoroughly, from breaking news to human-interest features. But one reporting flaw showed up in some stories—the estimate of how many Chinese nationals were being smuggled into the United States. Several stories quoted unnamed sources as saying "hundreds of thousands" of Chinese a year were being smuggled in. Ko-lin Chin, a Rutgers University sociologist who has studied the criminal smuggling trade, was then quoted in an Associated Press story this spring as saying he believes "10,000" Chinese a year entered the United States illegally.

Given official U.S. government estimates that 300,000 people enter the country illegally each year, most of them from Mexico and Central America, a figure of "hundreds of thousands" of Chinese is questionable. As a matter of politics, any number of illegal immigrants is problematic, but there is a considerable difference between a lower figure cited by a named source and the inflated numbers given by unnamed sources. Citing unconfirmed wild guesses by unnamed sources is irresponsible journalism.

In the area of labeling, journalism contributes to a confusion of identity of Asian Americans. This was most apparent in articles about Chinese food.

For example, the *New York Times* said, on Sept. 23, 1993, ("Restaurateurs Are Stung by a Study of Chinese Food"), "...the American customers had all but disappeared" from Chinese restaurants because of a study indicating Chinese food had a high fat content.

An Oct. 27, 1993, story in the *Washington Post*'s Food section on the same subject said, "The Chinese community was outraged and insulted by (the) study, although the bottom line was illuminating—that Chinese food, as ordered and eaten by Americans, may be higher in fat than one might have thought."

New York Times restaurant critic Ruth Reichl, in her March 18, 1994, "Dining in New York" column, wrote, "Most Chinese restaurants are so wary of American customers they don't even bother to offer them their best regional specialties."

American? Chinese? What is an "American"? Is it a racial-ethnic group? Or is it a national identity under which even ethnic Chinese who are American citizens can be embraced?

Some writers can't seem to avoid tiresome clichés or rhyming phrases when they talk about Asians and Asian American subjects. "Asian invasion" remains a sturdy favorite. This inflammatory phrase appeared regularly in different guises over the past year or two:

- "Show business: Hong Kong's Woo leads an Asian invasion" (*Time*, Sept. 13, 1993).
- "The Asian Invasion" (a headline in the *New Yorker*, above photos from recent Asian American and Asian-themed movies, March 31, 1994).
- "Movie Trends: Asian Invasion" (*Indianapolis Star*, Jan. 1, 1994).
- "A two-man Asian invasion has hit baseball" (*Sports Illustrated*, March 28, 1994).

Ironically, these headlines' "Asian invasion" imagery, which reinforces the stereotype of Asians as hostile foreigners, detracts from what were otherwise balanced articles about some aspect of the Asian American experience.

Cutesy phrases pop up in other articles. On Oct. 20, 1993, *New York Newsday* wrote in depth about the controversial study on fat in Chinese food. The main and sidebar stories were well reported. The headlines and graphics, however, bordered on trivializing clichés and mockery: "Much Ado About Moo Shu," "The Hot & Sour News About Chinese Food," "Chinese Food: Rice and Wrongs," "Take One from Column A."

In an otherwise insightful profile of Nike Chairman Phil Knight, Frank Deford (*Vanity Fair*, August 1993) resorted to cheap, stereotypical phrases. Example: "Even more, though, people who have studied him [Knight] say that his immersion in Japan and other places Asian has more particularly influenced him in his ability to be inscrutable and manipulative." Are Asians, as a racial group, the only people who are "inscrutable" and "manipulative?" Example: Knight "...replies without cracking even an Asian smile." Is there a European smile?

The underlying theme of such coverage is of Asians as exotica—witness reporting on the surprising success of Chinese women distance runners. In his *USA Today* sports column (Sept. 17, 1993), Tom Weir loaded up on clichés and stereotypes: "In China, 1993 is the Year of the Monkey. Fitting, because the Chinese are trying to play the rest of the sports world for chimps.... Confucius say that if Chinese are telling the truth [about a diet including turtle blood being partially responsible for world records]...hold off on that next order of Mao Tse-tongue."

Contrast Kenny Moore's precise reporting in *Sports Illustrated* (Sept. 27, 1993), and you have the difference between know-nothingness and solid journalism. Moore quoted several experts who cited demographics, youth and a punishing training regimen as the main reasons for the astonishing results of the Chinese women's team. And he didn't duck allegations of drug usage either.

The "mysterious Orient" hasn't vanished from the vocabulary of American journalism. ABC-TV's "Good Morning America" spent an early 1994 week in Hong Kong and showed, in its fashion, shallow features on various aspects of life there. But the white American hosts occasionally laced their chatter with references to "strange" and "mysterious" things. Strange and mysterious to whom?

Meanwhile, of course, plain old ignorance persists. In a Jan. 20, 1994, article in the Grand Rapids, Mich., *Press,* a story with the headline "Pseudo Sumos" about a new sports-bar "game" said the game makes a "mockery of the Oriental sport of sumo wrestling." Oriental? Sumo is a uniquely Japanese cultural form.

To some journalists, however, Asian Americans simply remain invisible. A spring 1994 article in the *Sacramento Bee,* headlined "Bid for UC Davis Chancellor/Push for more diversity may snag Vanderhoef's candidacy," reported that "there are currently no members of ethnic minorities at the helm of a UC campus." What about Chang-lin Tien, chancellor at the flagship Berkeley campus, who happens to be Chinese American?

Before five women were elected to the U.S. Senate in 1992 to bring the total female count to seven, a number of stories said the Senate was a "98-percent white male club." In a July 23, 1993, *New York Times* article about the only black female senator, Carol Moseley-Braun, Ben Nighthorse Campbell, the new senator from Colorado who happens to be a Northern Cheyenne Indian, was said to be "the Senate's only other nonwhite," which may have surprised Hawaii's senators, Daniel Inouye and Daniel Akaka.

In numerous stories that discuss American race relations, Asian Americans aren't mentioned, while Latinos (or Hispanics) are beginning to gain some notice and are breaking up the old black-and-white paradigm. One example was in a *New York Times* story about youth crime (May 18, 1994), which indirectly quoted a criminologist as saying, "One reason white gang members are not studied more is that they blend into the

American mainstream more easily than their black and brown counter-parts." Had Asian gangs, the former media favorite, suddenly disap-peared? And public opinion polls conducted by news organizations are notorious for leaving out Asian American views. Difficulty in gathering a statistically significant sampling of different Asian ethnic groups is a serious barrier to reflecting more diverse opinions, but those polls in regions of increasing Asian American presence should deepen efforts to include Asians.

Then there's just plain bad journalism. In a Santa Clarita, Calif., *Signal* article last year, headlined "Getting Oriented" (done up in a fake calligraphic font), writer Michael Klingbeil quotes a non-Japanese teacher of Japanese foreign students on Japanese marriage relationships. The teacher has culled "her knowledge from her intimacy with Japanese students over the years." The teacher said that a Japanese husband would slap his wife if she doesn't have his dinner ready for him when he gets home and would slap her again if she hasn't done the dishes. Those out-rageous generalizations should have been checked with Japanese cul-tural experts.

It is important to note the qualitative differences between print and broadcast coverage of Asian Americans. Some Asian American commu-nity activists in Los Angeles, for instance, have recently renewed com-plaints about how Los Angeles TV news stations ignore Asian Americans, except for sensational crimes, in a region that has seen tremendous growth in this population group.

Kathy Imahara, a civil rights attorney in Los Angeles, told *Asian Week* (June 3, 1994), "Los Angeles seems to have done a strange thing in [its] need to have an Asian woman anchor on all of the stations. I'm not sure where that's from. That hasn't, however, translated into any more stories about the Asian community."

American journalism need not expend extraordinary energy to fur-ther improve coverage of the Asian American population. It needs to use old standby tools of good reporting and precise writing with an extra dose of curiosity about apparent differences in cultures, real dif-ferences in languages.

Hiring more Asian American journalists couldn't hurt either, but edi-tors should use more than an ethnic criteria. They should look for, culti-vate and encourage Asian American journalists who bring special language and cultural skills. Filling an unstated quota with someone who happens to be of Asian descent but who has little special knowledge or skill isn't going to help cover the Asian American communities better.

In communities where Asian Americans now are more numerous, news organizations ought to assign reporters to cover the newcomers. Cultivating sources can be difficult but hardly impossible. Specialized language and cultural training for reporters would be money well spent. Asking lots of questions in different ways and showing respect for sources and learning about the new arrivals and not automatically imposing Western values on them should go a long way toward eradicating false notions, ignorance and insensitivity, without compromising journalistic values of fairness, balance and skepticism.

William Wong is a former columnist for the Oakland Tribune.

7

In the South—Press, Courts and Desegregation Revisited

Dale Thorn

As the latest higher education desegregation trial was about to get under way this spring in Mississippi, CNN broadcast a package illustrating the irony of these cases. CNN's report observed that years ago Mississippi blacks were suing to enter white colleges; today they were demonstrating to keep black colleges open.

"I just like being around more black people," a young black man, a student at Mississippi Valley State University, told a CNN reporter. A second black student, referring to Mississippi's Cleveland State University, with which the state wants to merge Mississippi Valley, lamented that "they have, you know, white people with Confederate flags on their trucks and stuff like that. You can't learn in an atmosphere like that."

In the next scene, CNN's coverage showed Benjamin Chavis Jr., executive director of the National Association for the Advancement of Colored People, leading the demonstration of 15,000 black students from around the nation. What CNN failed to report was that Chavis' presence signified a remarkable evolution on the part of the NAACP. Less than a decade previously, the NAACP had called for mergers of historically black and historically white public universities as the best way to ensure equal educational opportunity beyond high school. Toward the end of the 1980s, the group's position changed ever so slightly: The merger became just *one* means of ensuring equal educational opportunity. Today, on a warm spring day in Mississippi, a state under court order to dismantle the remaining vestiges of its dual higher education system, the NAACP had completed a 180-degree turn, opposing any mergers that would eviscerate a black college.

Compared to other groups, the speed of the NAACP's policy change was glacial. But the NAACP is not just any organization, but the one civil rights group that, more than any other, had embraced the premise of *Brown v. Board of Education*—that a separate education is inherently unequal. That was its premise when the Legal Defense Fund took the federal government to court in 1970. The lawsuit asked that the Department of Health, Education and Welfare make 10 Southern states adopt acceptable desegregation plans for higher education or cut off federal funds, in compliance with Title VI of the Civil Rights Act of 1964. At the time, more than 100 black college presidents argued, in opposition to the NAACP, that *Brown* did not apply to higher education. The NAACP wouldn't hear of it. Locally and nationally, it stood as a beacon to those who looked to *Brown* as requiring desegregation, not just race-neutral policies, throughout education. Now, in the year of *Brown*'s 40th anniversary, all that had changed. But no one would know it from mass media coverage.

Given the pressures of time on broadcast news, the networks' failure to provide this kind of context is perhaps understandable. CNN's failure is less understandable, given its all-news format. But even the printed press, on which we have come to rely for in-depth reporting of complex issues, has let us down. The otherwise solid reporting of the *Chronicle of Higher Education* hinted at the change, but failed to describe the NAACP's travails over time and how far it had come.

All too often, the media's reporting of legal cases based on history leaves us wanting more. Rarely can a reader or viewer learn from new accounts that the 19 states potentially affected by the mandate to desegregate higher education have one thing in common: All 19 states once had laws on the books *requiring* racially separate colleges for *both* blacks and whites. Geographically, the states range from the Deep South to Texas, Arkansas and Oklahoma in the Southwest, on to the Atlantic Coast states in the Southeast, and then to the border states and Ohio, Pennsylvania and Delaware. News consumers have had to rely on insiders and historians to put that story in perspective.

When Joseph A. Califano Jr., one of the insiders, became secretary of Health, Education and Welfare in 1977, he found the issues surrounding the legal mandate to desegregate higher education "as complex and subtle as any I faced."

Black colleges that had come into being after the Civil War provided opportunity to African-Americans who, "both discriminated against and badly instructed, couldn't get into even the least demanding white schools," Califano observed in his book *Governing America.*

Califano ultimately failed in his legal effort to deny federal funds to the University of North Carolina when it refused to go along with his approach of transferring academic programs from historically white to historically black campuses in order to encourage racial balance. North Carolina's battle with Califano and the federal bureaucracy received wide coverage. Viewed as prestigious in academe and progressive on race, North Carolina was expected to be a leader in dismantling the dual higher education system. And Califano knew that if he could break North Carolina, other Southern states would fall in line. But the coverage of the Califano-North Carolina confrontation in the early 1980s represented some of the most egregious, knee-jerk coverage ever seen in this arena. The media committed a number of errors that have colored much of the commentary on desegregation ever since.

These shortcomings in coverage date back to the *New York Times* editorial page of April 7, 1979. Under the headline "Still Separate in North Carolina," the *Times* made the reasonable call for further desegregation of the University of North Carolina. But in the same editorial, the paper reported that North Carolina and other Southern states had been ordered by a federal court "to end their dual systems of higher education or face the loss of federal funds." That had never happened. The federal court order in question chastised HEW for failing to enforce desegregation in 10 Southern states, but none of the states was ordered to do anything.

On July 11, 1981, the *Times* repeated the error but changed the dates. Under an editorial page headline "North Carolina's College Deal," the *Times* reported that the Legal Defense Fund had obtained desegregation orders against North Carolina's university system in 1974 and 1977. It never happened, in either year. But the Raleigh *News and Observer* reprinted the editorial, prompting U.S. District Judge Franklin T. Dupree, in a rare judicial notice of media coverage, to observe in a decision handed down in his North Carolina courtroom (*North Carolina v. U.S. Department of Education*) that the editorial was "simply erroneous." The *Times* had conveyed to its readers over a three-year period that the University of North Carolina had defied the law handed down in three court orders, when in fact no such edicts had been issued.

Perhaps feeding off the printed press, the popular CBS "Sunday Morning" program, then hosted by UNC graduate Charles Kuralt, aired a segment on the UNC case just two months later. CBS's 10-minute treatment included film of Gov. George Wallace, then a staunch segregationist, standing in the schoolhouse door at the University of Alabama in the early 1960s to block desegregation there, along with footage of federal troops marching onto a campus. Historian William Link, the biographer of UNC President William Friday, called the report "hostile," and Link was not alone. The *News and Observer*'s Claude Sitton, who had chronicled the civil rights movement for the *Times,* was no fan of the UNC board of governors, but even he pronounced the CBS presentation a "mugging." Responding to the furor, CBS gave President Friday five minutes on the air to respond on "Sunday Morning."

Amid the gaffes and stereotypes by the media elites, there has been a real dearth of relatively simple, interpretive, what-it-means reporting on the South's desegregation story. PBS's otherwise commendable "Eyes on the Prize II" failed even to mention higher education desegregation in the South. And in its all-too-brief review of the *Bakke v. Regents of the University of California* decision, "The Prize II" failed to point out that *Bakke* emanated from a state with no history of state-imposed (*de jure*) segregation in higher education. Thus, the U.S. Supreme Court decision in *Bakke,* holding that race may be a plus in the application file but not the sole factor in college admissions, does not apply to admissions decisions in the 19 states that once excluded students by law on the basis of race. In those states, despite *Bakke,* race may still be the decisive factor when used to overcome the *de jure* desegregation policy, a wrinkle the media missed.

Incisive, penetrating reporting to help the public understand these important distinctions would be especially helpful, from a regional perspective, in treating the substance and outcome of the court cases. Almost none of the reporting either in the South or by the national press has delved into the different means used to desegregate universities, but there is now enough data to draw some comparisons. In 1977, a federal court in Tennessee in *Geier v. Blanton* ordered a merger, the most radical remedy, of Tennessee State University and the University of Tennessee-Nashville, with the former to be the surviving institution. After considerable white flight, the court in 1984 set as a 1993 goal for Tennessee State a 50-50 racial mix, applied to students, faculty and staff, but most recent enrollment data indicate that white students make up about 32 percent of TSU's enrollment, despite the merger and a heavy infusion of capital improvements on the campus. The white flight in Tennessee was not the only testament to student sentiment—outside the courtroom at the 1984 hearing, a black protester carried a sign urging "Segregation and Justice for All."

North Carolina, which with five public historically black campuses has the most in the South, chose a different approach, refusing to merge institutions, close them or transfer academic programs between historically white and historically black campuses. Today at Fayetteville State, one of its historically black campuses, whites account for one-third of the enrollment. How did it happen? UNC officials say it was a case of a dynamic chancellor who embarked on genuine recruitment efforts, along with a sophisticated network of high school counselors and generous financial aid packages for deserving students.

That kind of remedy is clearly more subjective, more personality-oriented, more dependent upon good faith than the Tennessee solution. North Carolina's remedy, growing out of a consent decree after the state sued the federal government, has achieved about the same result at Fayetteville State as the Tennessee remedy did at Tennessee State, but at far less cost and with greater consensus. Conversely, when Louisiana signed a consent decree in 1981 (*U.S. v. Louisiana*), it called for the infusion of capital improvements and new degree programs at Southern University and Grambling State. When the decree expired six years later, a federal court concluded that the state's historically black campuses were more segregated than they had been before the decree. In effect, efforts to enhance the black campuses had made them more attractive to their traditional clientele: black students.

These kinds of state-to-state comparisons almost never appear in the mass media. Thus the casual reader, listener and viewer comes away from reports of a new court decision with the idea that there may be some magic-bullet approach to stimulate higher education desegregation when, in fact, different approaches over time may work in different ways in different places. Each state's media become absorbed in that state's case, and rarely does coverage cross state lines. Wire service coverage of one state's case seldom is picked up in another state facing the same issues because news editors frequently fail to see the significance of one case to the other.

If we take a more comprehensive look at what is happening across the various states, rather than look at each in isolation, we can learn more. And even when we focus on a single state, such as Mississippi, we can do better. Mississippi graduated 23,429 students from high school in 1992-93, according to its state Department of Education. Of that number, 67 percent pursued some form of postsecondary education. Of the 15,824 who chose college, 6,512 enrolled in four-year colleges, meaning that 9,312 went on to community or junior colleges, which are unaffected by the desegregation lawsuit. The media would provide a more precise perspective of *U.S. v. Fordice,* known in Mississippi as the *Ayers* case, if it shared this kind of information. Likewise, the media barely noticed when the U.S. Supreme Court in *Fordice* virtually invited states to close campuses. Addressing the dual higher education system for the first time since *Brown,* the Court in its 8–1 *Fordice* decision of 1992 concluded that the existence of eight senior universities "instead of some lesser number was undoubtedly occasioned by state laws forbidding the mingling of the races. And as the District Court recognized, continuing to maintain all eight universities in Mississippi is wasteful and irrational."

A woeful example of the media's myopia occurred in June 1993, when Atlanta newspapers ignored the Alabama desegregation case hearing in the 11th Circuit Court of Appeals in Atlanta, even for their Alabama edition. The *Montgomery Advertiser* also failed to report the hearing, even though Montgomery is home to the lead plaintiff in the case, state Rep. John F. Knight Jr., coordinator of communications and public affairs at Alabama State University. The *Advertiser* did run a wire service story, something the Atlanta papers failed to do, but the wire service coverage focused more on courtroom rhetoric than on the far-reaching issues.

The Alabama case, *Knight v. Alabama,* raised some issues not yet posed in other cases, and more compellingly than any case in the 1990s, despite the greater amount of ink and video the Mississippi lawsuit received. *Knight* looked beyond numbers. The case raised for the first time the quality of the racial climate on campuses and what would be taught in the desegregated setting. *Knight* came to the 11th Circuit after a nine-month district court trial that led to a 300-page opinion. Besides seeking $125 million for new buildings for Alabama State and Alabama A&M, the state's historically black campuses, Knight and his co-plaintiffs asked that the black institutions share "flagship" status with Auburn University and the University of Alabama and sought black studies programs and improved racial climates on the historically white campuses.

The district court had denied every major claim the Alabama plaintiffs put forth, except for the conclusion that the state had failed to eliminate the vestiges of segregation and that the two black campuses failed to share in state funding, both capital and operating, in an equitable manner. Instead of the requested $125 million for new buildings at the black campuses, the district court awarded $30 million. By prevailing on the liability question in the district court—the conclusion that remnants of segregation remained in the state's higher education system—Knight was awarded $1.9 million in attorney fees. But he wanted more than just money.

The 11th Circuit obliged, at least in remanding a number of critical issues for further consideration by the district court. Although it ruled against the somewhat nebulous bid for a better racial climate, the appellate court ordered the district court to re-examine the plaintiffs' inferior missions' claims on behalf of the two black campuses, as well as Alabama's decision to place all land-grant funds at Auburn rather than sharing them with Alabama A&M. But more basic, the appeals court particularly ordered another review of the plaintiffs' desire for more black studies programs on Alabama's white campuses. The district court should balance the curriculum claim with each faculty's First Amendment academic freedom interest in determining what will be taught, the 11th Circuit said. In each case, the court said, the district court must weigh the remaining vestiges of segregation, in accordance with *Fordice,* not on the basis of whether the state institutions have adopted and enforced race-neutral policies, but on the scales of whether the vestiges of segregation have continuing segregative effects and, if so, whether such effects "can be remedied in a manner that is practicable and educationally sound." In all cases, the burden of proof is on the state, because it once discriminated by statute.

Only slowly have the media come to realize that these cases represent not the simple Southern stereotype of governors barring the schoolhouse door to qualified students, but the complexity of bringing about some semblance of racial balance across an entire region and culture. At the same time, student choices must be truly free of discrimination, without the state artificially inhibiting those choices by the way in which *de jure* segregation historically distinguished institutions, their missions, their

academic programs and their budgets. Slowly, the media have come to
see not just the irony, but the complexity of the story as well.

U.S. District Judge Harold Murphy, in a part of his decision in the
Alabama case that has now been remanded for reconsideration, warned
that enhancing black colleges could carry a steep price. "The danger of
creating parallel universities in mission, one predominantly black, the
other predominantly white, cuts too close" to the separate-but-equal doc-
trine repudiated in *Brown,* Murphy wrote. In other words, the "Segregation and Justice for All" plea of the Nashville protester belongs to another
era, and so black campuses, born of segregation, are at risk. Ultimately,
the states must prove that those campuses either have no segregative
effects on society or that their elimination would be impractical and educationally unsound. That is a heavy burden for any state to bear—one
that Justice Antonin Scalia in his lone dissent in *Fordice* termed an "effectively unsustainable burden." As the states come to grips with it, higher
education desegregation becomes a story about as complex as any on the
domestic front.

In the days of the robust civil rights movement, the mass media were
called upon to provide coverage of what amounted to an appeal for simple
justice. Justice at that time entailed tearing down the walls of legal, state-
imposed segregation in almost every facet of public life. And the media
performed admirably. In the face of official efforts to silence the press,
New York Times v. Sullivan was but one testament to the national media's
courage and tenacity in exposing state-sponsored segregation. Today,
there are no states making concerted efforts to impede coverage of complex questions of civil justice. And, unlike the 1950s and '60s, what is at
issue now in the South is not coverage of simple justice, but of complex
justice. It would only add to the irony of the current university desegregation debate in the South if, at a time when the media were free to
extend coverage, they decided that the story was not adequately inviting.
What the media must realize is that *U.S. v. Fordice* is to public higher
education in the South what *Brown v. Board of Education* was to elementary and secondary schools in the region.

---

*Dale Thorn is an assistant professor in the Manship School of Mass Commu-
nication at Louisiana State University.*

8

Coloring the Crack Crisis

Jimmie L. Reeves and Richard Campbell

Technically speaking, cocaine is the principal psychoactive alkaloid of the coca leaf. Culturally speaking, however, the meaning of cocaine has undergone many revisions since the 1860s, when organic chemists first isolated the substance in the laboratory. In an age when cocaine has become condemned as a toxic contaminant—the killer of mighty athletes, the corrupter of admired politicians and the catalyst of frantic moral crusades—it is instructive to remember that in the 1870s and 1890s the substance was hailed as a wonder drug. Sigmund Freud, for instance, argued that cocaine, like caffeine, was helpful in the treatment of fatigue and nervousness—and even valuable as a cure for morphine addiction and alcoholism. During this period, Vin Mariani, a coca preparation marketed as a proprietary medicine, received enthusiastic endorsements from such figures as Thomas Edison, Pope Leo XIII, the Czar of Russia, Jules Verne, Emile Zola, Henrik Ibsen and the Prince of Wales.

Around the turn of the century, though, cocaine use increasingly became associated with an especially menacing form of modern deviant: the "dope fiend." But initial campaigns to make cocaine illegal were tainted by racism. For instance, in a 1903 report to the American Pharmacological Association, a committee on the Acquirement of the Drug Habit concluded that "the negroes, the lower and criminal classes are naturally most readily influenced" by cocaine. In keeping with contemporary trends in reporting, the press of yore contributed to the climate of racist hysteria surrounding the early regulation of cocaine, often using cocaine as a chemical scapegoat for the murder and mayhem that attended urban poverty in the early 1900s.

In the realm of the cultural, though, cocaine made something of a comeback in the late 1970s in terms of how the media portrayed the drug. Snorting the white powder form of cocaine became a rather naughty but generally socially acceptable display of conspicuous consumption that was as much a part of the mythical "Yuppie Way" as driving a silver BMW or sipping chilled Perrier. Over the course of the 1980s, however, the social meaning of cocaine again underwent radical shifts. Between 1981 and 1985, for instance, cocaine became increasingly known in the press and elsewhere as the drug of choice of the middle class, a mood-enhancing accessory of life in the fast lane. But in 1986, as drug experts and journalists discovered that small vials of crack priced within the means of the poor were becoming increasingly available in America's major metropolitan areas—New York, Los Angeles, Miami and Oakland, among others—these meanings would be almost completely inverted. As a packaging and merchandising innovation, crack secured a vastly expanded market for the legendary pleasures of cocaine—and as a spectacular news story of 1986, the crack legend would transform the meaning of cocaine from its status as the recreational drug of America's elite into the "desperational" drug of America's destitute.

In *Cracked Coverage,* our book-length study of 270 network television news reports broadcast between 1981 and 1988, we examine this latest struggle over the meaning of cocaine. The volume of cocaine stories rose dramatically during the decade before peaking in 1986. In 1987, TV news coverage dwindled a bit, only to rise again in the following presidential election year. Collectively, these reports form a kind of grand mosaic that may appropriately be called "The Reagan Era Cocaine Narrative." Like other major social and cultural controversies such as AIDS, abortion rights, television evangelism and environmental protection, the media's cocaine narrative at various moments expressed many of the prominent themes and antagonisms of the Reagan years: the meaning of cocaine would be inflected by class issues, take on racial overtones and would even animate myths about the sanctity of small-town life in Middle America.

Perhaps the chief finding of the larger study is our documentation of a disturbing disparity in the journalistic treatment of white "offenders" and black "delinquents" that jibes with racial politics of the Reagan coalition. In the early 1980s, when cocaine was seen as recreational and primarily associated with white "offenders," the approved purifying solution for the cocaine problem was therapeutic intervention. Most of the authorities on whom the media depended for sound bites in drug stories and to define the problem during this period were treatment experts working at private rehabilitation centers (e.g., psychologist Richard Miller of COKENDERS) or drug hotlines (e.g., Mark Gold and Arnold Washton of 800–COCAINE). The signature image of this coverage was of white, middle-class male cocaine "victims" in their late 20s, voicing the clichés of a cleansing confession during a group substance abuse therapy session ("I lost my home, I lost my wife, I lost my family, I lost my job," etc.). Like the rebirth rhetoric of Reaganism, then, the drug news of the early 1980s was heavily informed by the desire for recovery and the hope of rehabilitation. As Joanne Morreale, a campaign media analyst, puts it, "Reagan's rebirth rhetoric offered secular salvation, a symbolic resolution of personal and public crises."

Journalism's discovery of crack in late 1985 signalled the beginning of a period of frenzied coverage in which the race and class contours of the cocaine problem established in the early 1980s would be almost completely reconfigured: What was once defined as a glamour drug and decadent white transgression became increasingly associated with pathology and poor people of color isolated in America's inner cities—the so-called urban underclass. During this crisis period, the approved journalistic solution to the drug problem was no longer therapeutic intervention devoted to individual rehabilitation and recovery. Instead, crack coverage favored modes of exclusion enforced by the three P's of the hard sector of the drug control establishment—police, prosecution and prison. While most of the primary definers of coverage in the early 1980s had been treatment experts, once the crack crisis broke, crusading politicians (such as President Ronald Reagan and U.S. Rep. Charles Rangel, D-NY) and aggressive law enforcement officials (including DEA agent Robert Stutman, Maryland State Prosecutor Arthur Marshall and New York Police Commissioner Benjamin Ward) assumed much more prominent roles in framing the crisis. Instead of the compassionate tone laced with the hope of recovery that had typified response to cocaine in the early part of the decade, the crack crisis helped promote a new racist backlash that justified the symbolic criminalization of a generation of black youth.

One of the most important developments that facilitated this coloring of the news framing of cocaine coverage in 1986 was the journalistic discovery and demonization of a deviant setting that became depicted as nothing less than a locus of evil in our culture and our neighborhoods—the crack house. A threatening place of assembly and enterprise, the crack house was often depicted as territory in which the entrepreneurial spirit and the ideology of consumerism (that are so central to Reagan-omics) are pushed beyond the limits of decency, good taste and social and moral control. Indeed, the characters who frequented the crack house were often described, even in their own public confessions, as "out of control." But perhaps the most damning thing about the crack house is its association with an underground economy, a "black market" that embraces the central principles of capitalism, most notably the profit motive, while also undermining the legitimate economy's longstanding efforts to discipline its work force. As sociologist Todd Gitlin observes, America is a drug culture:

> Through its normal routines it promotes not only the high-intensity consumption of commodities but also the idea that the self is realized through consumption. It is addicted to acquisition. It cultivates the pursuit of thrills; it elevates the pursuit of pleasure to high standing; and, as part of this ensemble, it promotes the use of licit chemicals for stimulation, intoxication, and fast relief. The widespread use of licit drugs in America can be understood as part of this larger set of values and activities.

In a round-about way, by giving concrete form to the limits and the contradictions of "this larger set of values and activities," the crack house plays an important role in the maintenance of contemporary mainstream institutions and manners. In the crack house setting, we see the despair, the exploitation and the perversity of capitalism writ large: consumerism over the edge.

Or Reaganomics out of control.

Journalism's obsession with the site of the crack house as abnormal or deviant space, then, masks the actual ways the crack house mimics the normal and routine business workings of capitalist enterprise.

The vilification of the crack house as a sinister place of assembly has, of course, justified the most brutal and excessive of armed responses by the forces of decency and control. In these purifying expeditions into the chaos and filth of the crack house, the network news frequently has en-couraged strong audience identification with the crusading police. In such "reality-based" reports, the journalist often literally adopts the outlook of the police—a perspective that, in the context of the inner city, is per-haps best described as the colonizer's point of view on the colonized.

This angle of journalistic identification often features the use of the clandestine camera. In television news, the use of a clandestine camera is almost always associated with stigmatization—the John DeLorean sting or the arrest of Washington Mayor Marion Barry on drug charges, for example. The clandestine camera marks the transgressor under surveillance as an alien "Other" who does not have the same rights to privacy accorded ordinary citizens. In our book, we distinguish between two types of clandestine footage—"independent" and "implicated." The former is footage gathered by news organizations without the cooperation of policing authorities: Footage that uses a hidden camera to record open drug transactions on the mean streets of large U.S. cities, for example. Implicated footage, on the other hand, is material that can be gathered only with the cooperation of law enforcement organizations. In some cases, this footage involves journalists taking cameras along on police sting operations and recording the action; in others, the footage may actually be generated by government surveillance cameras and then incorporated into the reporter's news package, such as the prosecution's footage of Marion Barry in that Washington hotel room.

The percentage of cocaine stories featuring clandestine footage rises over the course of the 1980s. In our video sample of coverage between 1981 and 1985, only about one story in four (11 out of 42) would feature such footage—but in 1987 and 1988, such footage appears in over half the cocaine stories (27 of 48) we analyzed. But the most striking development in stigmatizing camera work occurred during the 1986 crack crisis coverage—the emergence of the raiding footage of a hand-held camera accompanying police forces during the invasion of a crack house. This raiding footage does not appear at all in cocaine coverage of the early 1980s (when cocaine was treated as a "white" problem). But beginning with an ABC news report on July 28, 1986, it became a titillating feature of several TV network drug crisis updates. As DEA agent Stutman observed, it was easy to enlist journalists in the war on drugs because crack was "the hottest combat-reporting story to come along since the end of the Vietnam War." In the post-crisis coverage, as raiding footage became incorporated into the "image bank" available for recycling in any network news story about cocaine, it became something of a visual cliché, appearing in about one out of every four stories in our video sample.

For us, raiding footage represents nothing less than the convergence of the reportorial outlook with the policing point of view. In this convergence, we observe a shift to a proactive strategy in press/police relations, a strategy that would pay off during the 1980s war on drugs in favorable coverage of high-profile drug campaigns choreographed for the television cameras by police organizations in San Francisco on CBS in August 1981, in San Diego on ABC in March 1984, in New York City on CBS in August 1986 and March 1988, in Miami on ABC in July 1986, in Miami on NBC in August 1986 and November 1987, and in New Jersey on CBS in September 1986.

In its coverage of drugs and inner-city America during the Reagan era, conventional journalism provided plenty of description, information, cautionary tales and horror stories. But the public debates over the racial and class dimensions of drugs, over legalization and, especially, over the costs of supporting the expanding police state remained suppressed by media hysteria that succeeded only in manufacturing an apparent national consensus on drug matters: "Just say no." (For the record, for every cocaine- or crack-related death in the United States, there are approximately 300 deaths associated with nicotine and 100 with alcohol.)

Given such crusading journalists, operating under the auspices of professional neutrality and leading consensus-building, it was no great surprise when on April 29, 1992, the four Los Angeles police officers were acquitted in the Rodney King beating case; as one of the lawyers for the four officers told the *New York Times,* he had been able "to put the jurors in the shoes of the police officers." Indeed, with the surge of stories about crack cocaine in inner-city America, TV news since late 1985 had been doing much the same thing as that L.A. defense lawyer—putting mainstream America into the shoes of the police. In the routine, ritualized visual imagery of TV crack coverage—the unstable, hand-held camera bounding from the back of police vans following gun-toting authorities as they break down the door of yet another crack house—journalism became an agent of the police, putting Americans, sitting in the comfort of their living rooms, into "the shoes of the police."

Ultimately, our larger study concludes that, in authorizing and advocating the New Right's anti-drug activism, drug experts and network journalists operated as moral entrepreneurs in the political economy of Ronald Reagan's America—entrepreneurs who benefited personally and professionally from co-producing a series of moral panics that centered around controlling this stuff called cocaine and disciplining the people who used it. By adopting a "support the troops" mentality in their promotion of the war on drugs, drug experts and journalists were not simply involved in disseminating the disciplinary wisdom of "just saying no." Instead, they were also deeply implicated in advancing, even mainstreaming, the reactionary backlash politics of the New Right in a way that helped mask the economic devastation of deindustrialization, aggravated white-black tensions and, ultimately, helped solidify middle-class support for policies that favored the rich over the poor.

While we do not expect that these conclusions will be at all convincing to drug warriors, we do think they are compelling enough to make most thoughtful readers re-evaluate journalistic performance in the area of coverage of drugs and, more broadly, race during the 1980s. But, perhaps even more importantly, we hope our findings are persuasive enough to force thoughtful journalists to reconsider: 1) how reporters deal with government officials and enterprising experts who have vested interests in cultivating drug hysteria; and 2) how reporters routinely mark off certain segments of the population as deviants who are beyond rehabilitation.

Jimmie L. Reeves and Richard Campbell are co-authors of Cracked Coverage: Television News, the Anti-Cocaine Crusade, and the Reagan Legacy *(1994), from which parts of this essay are adapted.*

III

Issues, Debates and Dilemmas

9

Are the Media Really "White"?

Andrew Hacker

No one raises objections when *Ebony* and *Essence* are described as black magazines, or that Black Entertainment Television bears a racial designation. We all know that Carl Rowan and Clarence Page are black columnists. In a similar vein, several schools with journalism programs choose to call themselves historically black institutions.

But suppose it were proposed that the *Los Angeles Times* or the *New Republic* be characterized as "white" publications. Or that we refer to ABC and PBS as "white" networks, and from now on speak of Ellen Goodman and George Will as "white" journalists. And, for good measure, identify Columbia and most other journalism schools as "historically white."

Reactions to such suggestions may be readily predicted. To start, we may be told, not all of reality divides into polar opposites. Just because *Ebony* and Rowan and Tuskegee are viewed as black, it need not mean that Goodman and the *New Republic* and ABC must be counterpoised as "white." (Hence the inclination to surround "white" with quotation marks, but not to do so with black.) Thus, the mainstream media, like other major institutions, reject any racial label as irrelevant and inappropriate. This is not to deny that columnists like Goodman and Will willingly grant that they "happen" to be white, just as a network will aver that this is the case with most of its employees. But these individuals and organizations would probably cite other elements in their makeup that are even more essential to their identities. Why, they might ask, should race be seen as the central feature of diverse media systems and complex personalities?

And CBS might reply that its "60 Minutes" gives Ed Bradley equal billing with Mike Wallace, while the powers that be at NBC could cite Bryant Gumbel's popularity with the dominantly white audience that tunes in to "Today." Given the nation's mosaic, it would be odd indeed if we encountered an outright refusal to hire a Connie Chung or a Geraldo Rivera. In fact, we will be told, the point is not whether all races are represented, but that race is immaterial. Thus *Business Week* might challenge anyone to show how its coverage of corporate buyouts contains an ethnic bias.

These responses are sincerely stated, even if no one senses an undue defensiveness. Moreover, these sentiments are not confined to those working in the media. As it happens, the 200 million or so Americans who carry the majority pigmentation seldom think of themselves as "white." (This is the last time quotation marks will be used.) While they have no objection to checking that box on a form, they will add that they give more thought to specific aspects of their identity, like Italian or Scottish or Jewish origins. The white designation may fit egregious exceptions like neo-Nazis and the Ku Klux Klan, but imagine the sputtering if a station decided to bill itself as the White Entertainment Television.

Indeed, those who see the world through white eyes will assert that they are unable to think of any traits or attributes that all Caucasians have in common. While there is still general agreement that the nation's official antecedents are European, as are its reliance on Western literature and learning, this is seen as a cultural, not a racial, heritage. Just as most white Americans protest that the charge of racism does not apply to them, so they also deny the centrality of their race. Nor does it occur to them that there might be a connection between these two disavowals.

Most Americans of African ancestry take a very different view. In their perception, the dominant media are most certainly white, with no need for quotation marks. To their eyes, the mainstream media speak for a white nation, which expects all citizens to conform to its ways. Nor do they see that much has changed since the Kerner Commission remarked, "The media report and write from the standpoint of a white man's world." For starters, those who wish to move ahead in this world should do their best to emulate white demeanor and diction. And this in turn means that black Americans should cast themselves as the kinds of people whites would like blacks to be.

Needless to say, white Americans find it unsettling that black citizens see things this way. Most whites want to feel that they have made genuine overtures, and they tell of acquaintances and workmates with whom they get on well. This is especially evident in sectors of the media where liberal sentiments prevail.

Is this simply a case of miscommunication, to be threshed out in a workshop or seminar or weekend retreat? Come now. What these black colleagues see is a reality: that for the greater part of their lives, they have been confined to a separate sphere. Save for some marginal mingling, whites live among whites, and blacks among blacks. Due to the persistence of this segregation, which for blacks is partly voluntary but ultimately imposed, the two nations have evolved distinctive cultures. The racial division holds at every class level, so much that even black Ivy League alumni schedule separate reunions because they feel out of place among white classmates.

Hence, too, the necessity for a handbook like Anita Doreen Diggs' *Success At Work: A Guide for African Americans* (Barricade Books, 1993), which opens with the warning: "The first rule is: learn how to get along with white people." This is not easily achieved, as is made clear in her exercise in applied anthropology. Nor, she tells her black readers, should they expect reciprocity. She shows how white colleagues and supervisors feel no obligation to recognize black styles and sensibilities, let alone acknowledge that they exist. "Remain calm," she advises, "even in the face of extreme provocation."

Like many other enterprises, most media organizations will assert that they want more minorities on their rosters, adding that they have made serious recruitment efforts. However, they continue, the pool of qualified candidates is depressingly small, due to causes that often begin at birth. Furthermore, journalism finds itself competing with other fields, many of which can offer better starting salaries or prospects for promotion.

All will agree that many kinds of talents are looked for in reporters and editors and producers, from technical proficiency and social skills to an intuitive flair for understanding events. Nor is there a single model. But there is an additional trait, one seldom openly mentioned, that is looked for in colleagues who are black. It goes beyond whether they will "fit in" congenially, since that question also arises regarding whites. Frankly stated, what those on board want to know is whether a black candidate will turn out to be hostile, political, resentful and hence likely to be unhappy with his or her assignments and surroundings.

Not far beneath the surface is an image—more accurately, a fantasy—of the ideal black workmate. Needless to say, he or she adapts readily to the company of whites, and has no problem with being the only black in a room. This colleague should also smile a great deal, which puts whites at their ease, as well as show gratitude for having been hired. Or, as Diggs puts it, "you need to hold your tongue, tread lightly, and dodge the delicate issue of race." If the topic does arise, the model workmate will assure those present that they are not culpable. As a further earnest, it is best to go on record opposing figures whites regard as divisive or demagogic. In short, every media organization wants replicas of Colin Powell and Hazel O'Leary.

That all major media have predominantly white audiences is a bottom line that black employees are expected to understand and appreciate. At the same time, they are largely hired to cover race-based assignments. After all, one doesn't usually send white reporters to Nation of Islam conventions or inner-city interviews. Even here, though, the stories must be pitched to white readers, in ways whites can square with their preconceptions and perceptions. (Ed Bradley comes across as the consummate model.) Most black workers in the media feel there is a reality out there that they are unable to report. Of course, events are recorded and issues are raised, but only after they have been sufficiently distilled to be palatable to white readers and viewers. This may explain why so many black journalists—Brent Staples, Ellis Cose, Nathan McCall, Jill Nelson—have taken time off to write books in which they can say what they want in their own way.

What, then, of all the talk of our being a multicultural country, with acceptance and respect for people who do not look or sound like ourselves? Our children are being taught about Cherokee customs, Colombian cuisines and Korean contributions to our nation's life. The 1990 census found that Americans with European origins had fallen to three-quarters of the population, a decline that is bound to continue. This being the case, one might expect that the major media would reconsider their attitudes and approaches.

Or perhaps not. Instead, they may feel that differences based on origin are less crucial than one might think, and tend to be transitory. In fact, the great majority of newcomers have come here intending to adapt to the white cultural model. This process is already under way among millions of Hispanics and Asians, who are readying themselves to be co-opted by white institutions. So it is not surprising that black Americans are called upon to emulate immigrants' aspirations. Yet the irony and tragedy is that people whose forebears have been here for almost four centuries are made to carry a heavier burden of proof than even recent arrivals. This would suggest that a belief persists that no matter what tests individuals of African origin may pass, a belief persists that they will still lack the requisites for full absorption into a society that claims to exalt diversity and opportunity.

Andrew Hacker is professor of political science at Queens College in New York City. A new edition of his book Two Nations: Black and White, Separate, Hostile, Unequal *was released by Ballantine in 1995.*

10

Warping the World—Media's Mangled Images of Race

Jannette L. Dates and Edward C. Pease

Whenever the media cover events or develop new entertainments ve-hicles that involve race in any form—from O.J. Simpson to "Fresh Prince" to immigration policy to "The Joy Luck Club" to the Nation of Islam to South Central L.A.—something "happens" to their heads. Or, if it doesn't, something should. In the case of such media offerings, which *must* in-volve race in an increasingly diverse America, the ante of audience per-ception rises and the keepers of the media gates—most of whom are from the white, male "mainstream"—tense up. Somewhere, however deep down, they know that many of their viewers, readers and listeners are not like them, neither white nor male, and see the world differently. And, at the opposite end of the media chain, minority audience members tense up as well when they turn on the television or pick up the newspaper, be-cause they know the images and messages about themselves and their communities they will see and hear are shaped (and misshaped) by white people.

As this journal discusses and others fully document elsewhere, the norm in this country is that the perspectives of white, mainstream men generally create the lenses through which America—whether peripher-ally or directly—views race, and itself. Thus, there is good reason for many minorities— African Americans, Latinos, Asian Americans, Na-tive Americans and non-Caucasian ethnic immigrants who are not part of "mainstream" white America—to think their perspectives are at best warped by the media or, worse, not heard at all. In the year that saw a black man elected president of South Africa, there is irony that apartheid still rules the information age in America.

In a democratic society founded on the premise that an open flow of information is crucial if the populace is to make just, fair and informed decisions, such distortions and omissions in the totality of media content—from advertising to entertainment to news—can wreak havoc on the American population and on how well the media serve society's represented and unrepresented alike. By definition, information whose sources are limited—whether by political outlook, economic status, education, gender, age or race—is of fatally limited value to a society founded upon diversity of opinion and informed decision-making. News of politics, the economy or social developments sheds a dim light for the larger society if it lacks an understanding of "other" groups, if it focuses on any segment to the exclusion of any others.

This is hardly a new idea, although it has been one difficult to effect. In 1947, the Hutchins Commission report on *A Free and Responsible Press* urged the news media to promote public discussions on important issues and to help ensure that all community elements have opportunities to express their views. The Hutchins report called for a "truthful, comprehensive and intelligent account of the day's events in a context which gives them meaning," and for the press to take care to provide society a representative picture of its constituent parts. The responsibility of a free and open media in a free and open society, the Commission said, was to provide the means for the members of that society to talk to each other. Twenty years later, little had changed. The Kerner Commission, established by President Lyndon B. Johnson after the civil disorders of the mid-1960s, severely criticized the nation's media for failing to transmit information adequately about race relations and ghetto problems and urged the media to " bring more Black people into journalism" in order to make that possible.

Even today, more than four decades after Hutchins, it seems such a simple task, and remains such an elusive goal.

Part of the alienation from mainstream media found in South Central Los Angeles, Harlem, the South Side of Chicago and other racially and culturally bounded neighborhoods springs form a distrust learned of experience. People know that the system discourages people like them from sharing their perceptions of the day's events. They know that the world as it appears in mainstream news and entertainment in America is nearly always strained through the cultural filters that white decision-makers—however well-meaning—believe reflect "the" reality or "the" truth, and is absorbed by audiences that wear the same perceptual blinders. Interpretations of events that do not conform to the gatekeepers' worldview fade out as if they never existed. And society's "others," who may see the world differently, are just as effectively filtered out of the media's version of "reality." ABC's Ted Koppel, for example, conceded that his "Nightline" show visited South Africa for the first time in 1985 after years of lobbying by black ABC employees; that week's "Nightline," anchored in South Africa by Kenneth R. Walker, an African American, became one of the most lauded news reports in the history of broadcast journalism. Meanwhile, however, on a day-to-day basis, most viewers of American TV news know black men only as criminals, and people of color as poor, desperate or dangerous. That is the media's warped reality of the world in the 1990s. "The offering pattern has African Americans disproportionately included in negative coverage—as prostitutes, drug dealers, welfare recipients, second-story men, unwed mothers," observed *Newsday*'s Les Payne. "It's a strange place, this black world the media project."

Walter Lippmann, recognizing the importance of cultural forces in society, once noted that "the subtlest and most pervasive of influences are those which create and maintain the repertory of stereotypes. We are told about the world before we see it. We imagine most things before we experience them. And those preconceptions, unless education has made us acutely aware, govern deeply the whole process of perception."

Perceptions, always dangerous and rarely true, cut in many directions. Perception of race, for instance, is rarely a true rudder. As we end the 20th century, young people (and older) are taught—largely through media repetitions of social myths, misconceptions, stupidity and outright bigotry—to view people as types locked into certain stereotypical, inalterable (and inaccurate) modes. Puerto Ricans are oily and drive Chevies with loud stereos. Black women are single mothers on welfare; black men are violent. Asians (any variety) are inscrutable (and good at math). Mexicans are in this country illegally and have large families to support. White men are successful, happy and drive BMWs. And so on. The media project images of each of these groups and others that create, reinforce and perpetuate popular "knowledge" of them that rarely is grounded in reality, "knowledge" on which members of those groups themselves as

well as others in society form judgments and act. It is a dangerous, divisive and wasteful world that the media create.

Those media, which as has been said operate from the perspective of a
white man's world (especially television, but also newspapers and
newsmagazines, films and books), have long taught audiences to fear black
men. The poet Sterling Brown sees seven types of black characters in
modern American media, and suggests that blacks are routinely viewed
via media representations in classifications that range from those that will
reassure a white audience—the "contented slave," the "comic buffoon"
and even the "exotic primitive"—to those that confirm their worst fears—
the "wretched freedman," the "tragic mulatto" and the "savage brute."

At the end of the 20th century in the United States, the problems of
inner-city African Americans are exacerbated as impressionable young
people absorb the pervasive and persuasive imagery of what society
expects of them that is promoted in print, broadcast and other media.
Imagine yourself a young black man of 16 named James. Or a woman
named Janelle. You are a high school junior with an interest in, say,
literature or maybe mathematics. You're thinking about college and a
career in, say, engineering, maybe medicine. But when you watch TV,
listen to the ratio, read the newspaper, you can see yourself only in
another, more limiting light. Via the media, most of the people you see
who are like you resemble Brown's "savage brute," with all the pathological behavior that label implies. It is a vision of "reality" that is
documented and reiterated daily both for you and people like you—as
well as for people who aren't—in the news and entertainment media, in
accounts of gang killings, drug busts, teen-age pregnancies, street-smart
kids on the make, in newspapers, magazines, TV news and more. Or,
perhaps you see people like you portrayed as Brown's "comic buffoon," as blacks so often appear in movies or TV sitcoms, the main
vehicles by which the dominant culture defines African Americans in
prime time. Almost never would you see yourself in either news or
entertainment in a role that falls between he extremes of brute and
clown—Mike Tyson and Fox TV's "Martin." Neither would you be
likely to see yourself in positions of responsibility—as news anchors,
correspondents, commentators or producers. Nor will you see yourself
in thoughtful entertainment formats where issues of serious concern
are addressed in a realistic and meaningful way. When the dominant
voices of authority and respect that James or Janelle sees, hears and

reads, represented in the media as the smartest, most resourceful, most attractive most competent and courageous, are always white men, then even the strongest of "others" must feel dismissed and devalued.

As a result of this kind of acculturation, and because solid information about minority contributors and thinkers is so seldom included in their education, many young blacks, Hispanics and Asians are rendered unable to believe in their own society—a culture in which they and their closest contemporaries appear to have had so little part in developing in the past, and so little prospect of controlling in the future. And, just as tragic, white audiences receiving those same messages can't see much of a place for James or Janelle, either.

If media gatekeepers are generally white and male, it is not so surprising that the messages they permit to pass through their media gate support their own views of the world, nor that that view is based on a concept of white male supremacy that they, too, have been taught. It is also not surprising that these gatekeepers are not as likely to let pass alternative views—of James/Janelle, say, of an African-American or Latino experience and the perspectives that inform their worldviews. The result may be white supremacist images in the mass media that become interwoven in the fabric of popular culture, images that are instrumental in molding public opinion, influencing discussion about racial differences, and influencing action.

Because they reflect and transmit society's predominant values and ideology, mass media images help to define the collective experience, shape social consciousness, and serve to legitimate current conditions. In America, the negative images of African Americans and other minorities that evolve in society in general and in the media in particular images most people accept as authentic. These images have negative consequences both in terms of those groups' own self-image and white perspectives of them.

Some African Americans, along with the white decision-makers who control the media industries, are making money—and a lot of it—in a widespread use of television and motion pictures that defines black people in ways that are more destructive than any ever seen. What we see in the media of the 1990s are modern-era minstrel shows (sitcoms), movie thrillers, rap music and music videos that celebrate misogyny and violence, and that communicate parodied images of black men, shucking and jiving con artists who joke about pathological behaviors and criminality, while playing the role of black "bucks" to a white America. In the end, such images and attitudes diminish black and white Americans alike.

Jannette L. Dates is acting dean of the School of Communications at Howard University in Washington, D.C., and co-author of Split Image: African Americans in the Mass Media (1994). *Edward C. Pease is chair of the Department of Communication at Utah State University.*

11

Pop Culture, "Gangsta Rap" and the "New Vaudeville"

Paul Delaney

Black Americans and other nonwhites have always been, with good reason, nervous about how white Americans perceive them. From the beginning, we imitated the dominant society in dress, dance, culture— whether we took those styles seriously or mocked them. We knew that white perceptions of how well we could "fit in" made a huge difference in our lives, determining our role and status in this country—which of us would be field or house slaves and who would rise to company vice presidency. Obviously, the media play a vital role in shaping and per- petuating perceptions, helping whites to make up their minds on how well we "fit in."

That is why African Americans have so zealously kept vigil on what the media say about us. On many occasions, it has seemed an overreac- tion; at times, such vigilance and sensitivity have even been the subject of debate within the black community itself. At the turn of the century, there was deep division among African Americans over the philosophies of Booker T. Washington and W.E.B. Du Bois on which way to proceed following *Plessy v. Ferguson.* During the 1960s, there was a split be- tween the moderates of the National Association for the Advancement of Colored People and more militant organizations over the course of the civil rights movement.

There have been serious differences within the black community over social, cultural and religious issues, as well. Many a blues artist who started out singing in the church choir had to overcome strong family objections to performing "Satan's music." Adults in the 1950s complained about dirty and suggestive words in a lot of doo-wop songs: the entire "Annie" series of recordings by Hank Ballard and the Midnighters—for example, "Work With Me Annie" and "Annie Had a Baby," as well as their "Sexy Ways." Meanwhile, of course, white parents had to contend with gyrations from Elvis Presley, music from the "free love" 1960s and since.

The latest such musical upheaval is rap. Gangsta rap, to be more precise, since rap music in general is no better or worse than the offerings of the 1950s and 1960s. Defenders of rap are correct in one thing, that the music mirrors serious urban problems and may be a plea, a warning, to do something about them. Rap came along after the convergence of a host of powerful and sometimes conflicting phenomena: The civil rights movement and the progress that resulted, and then the ensuing backlash. The sexual revolution. Women's lib. Then came hard-earned black successes in the media, especially on television and in the entertainment industry, and the fact that much of blacks' exposure and success has been no better or worse than TV fare in general—that is, terminally stupid sitcoms and the "new vaudeville." With this emerged the shallowness of television, at odds with its awesome potential and power; justifiable concern for a First Amendment in conflict with creativity and increasing violence and gratuitous sex on the screen, declining quality of news programming and the tabloidization of news in both print and broadcast media.

Finally, and most important for blacks, television's influence eventually came to overwhelm traditional sources of authority in the community—parents and neighbors, the church, educators and civil rights and community leaders. (This is not to say that negative influence did not also extend to white communities, but its impact on an already embattled, insecure black community was more devastating.) Those traditional, individual and community-based sources of taste, decorum, mores, habits and the full range of social behavior and codes were overpowered by mass communication and modern American life. Where many, if not the majority of, black parents used to wield influence over what their children did, over which personal, cultural and community forces would be emphasized, it is virtually impossible for them to do so nowadays.

There are other forces, including the relationship between black consumers and television, and images of blacks in and on television, that have put blacks in a box, a position that is nothing new. On the one hand, there is genuine pride in the fact that recent times have been good to and for blacks in TV as stars, producers, directors—jobs previously denied to them because of race. But, there is also strong objection to many of the roles and images transmitted—including the clown image of the "new vaudevillians," but particularly the messages of gangsta rappers about women as "bitches" and "hos," about guns and violence and cops.

Headlines highlight the issues: "Must Blacks Be Buffoons?" *Newsweek* asked. "Black Life on TV: Realism or Stereotypes?" posed the *New York Times*. Have we come all the way from the Harlem Renaissance to the civil rights movement, from colored to Negro to black to African American, from black and proud and "We shall overcome," only to arrive at black culture characterized by "bitches" and "hos" on the airwaves and over the counter in record stores?

Along the way, there has been a significant shift in the feelings and responses of white Americans to race. I need not detail the contributions of the Ronald Reagan and George Bush campaigns and administrations, which pandered to racism, details conveniently overlooked nowadays by many political and social commentators. Reagan set the stage for much of what followed in racial terms in America in the 1980s and 1990s with his obscene presidential campaign-opener in 1979 in—of all places— Philadelphia, Miss. Before that came Richard Nixon and his "Southern strategy," and George Wallace stirring the racial pot.

No matter the grievances and their causes, however, there was no justification for gangsta rappers to go on a binge against women. Bushwick Bill of the Geto Boys defended his own use of "bitches" and "hos" by explaining that he was brought up to think of women in those terms—as if this were reason enough. He told this to a workshop audience at last year's convention of the National Association of Black Journalists in Houston. Several hundred women, and their male supporters, walked out.

"What arrested emotional development has led so many young black men to feel this way (or at any rate support those who do)?" asked William Raspberry, Pulitzer Prize-winning columnist of the *Washington Post*. "What self-contempt has led so many young black women to go along with it? What perversion of priorities has led the rest of us to ignore it for so long?"

(My own answer, without benefit of scientific studies or data, is that there seems to be none. After a career of covering social problems, I know that there exists a widespread and seething contempt for women among many inner-city, young black men, the result of being born to struggling single or teen-aged mothers with boyfriends in and out of their homes and beds, many times with children in the same room, something sons in particular find contemptible and, I believe, leaves terrible emotional scars and a permanent resentment toward women.)

Historically, blacks had little control over the way whites perceived them, but they did influence the actions and activities of their own children and community. Hence the concern about image and preventing those white perceptions of blacks from dominating black youth and black community, and so the battles against "Birth of a Nation" and blackface comedy and "Amos 'n' Andy."

Author Mel Watkins deals with these and other issues of black images in his fine book (with the seemingly interminable title), *On The Real Side: Laughing, Lying, and Signifying—The Underground Tradition of African-American Humor That Transformed American Culture, From Slavery to Richard Pryor.*

"While white society had geared itself to resist advances by blacks in employment, voting, housing, and union affiliation," he wrote, "there were fewer obstacles to blacks in publishing and entertainment." (To which I would add that whites have never objected to being entertained by blacks.) "There, they felt the battle for racial equality could best be fought by presenting a more complete view of black life and by demonstrating that blacks could make worthwhile contributions to higher culture."

Watkins' point reminds me of a sincere belief among some blacks a generation ago that integrated sports, both college and professional, would soften white attitudes about us and lead to our salvation. This view was prevalent especially among some black sports editors, including the late Marion Jackson of the *Atlanta Daily World,* where I worked at the time. I disagreed totally and spent many drinking sessions arguing the point with him.

In his book, Mel Watkins traces the development of black comedy, noting that black contributions were largely ignored and that only recently—since the 1960s—could white Americans tolerate being the brunt of biting humor by black comedians, preferring, he says, "a less truculent, more polite middle-class demeanor." Eventually, the likes of Redd Foxx, Flip Wilson and Richard Pryor, among others, changed that. And now, we have gangsta rappers, with their in-your-face realism, putting on compact disc what was previously reserved for the privacy of the parlor or the plain brown wrapper, the street corner or under-the-table record sales. What this boils down to is that if playing the dozens were still on the corner, if calling women "bitches" and "ho's" remained behind closed doors instead of nightly offerings on cable and HBO and on CDs, and on loudspeakers of the car in the next lane (or a block away— "In your face, everybody!"), if the electronic media were not so powerful, pervasive and influential, if we were only back in the 1940s (as a lot of Americans wish), if Amos 'n' Andy were as innocent as some believe—if all the above and more were so, we would not be having this debate today.

It is fascinating that the flap over harsh language and gangsta rap rages most ferociously in the black community. Whites look on from the sidelines, like innocent bystanders. Yet, most of the financial benefits go to white record company owners, white marketing experts, white producers, etc., and more white kids buy and listen to rap music than do black youngsters. Many blacks are cynical about the new fad, convinced that when white youngsters grow up or tire of the music or it is time to get serious about life, they can pull the plug on rap, go back to the safety and security of suburbia and the family business or their own professional careers and live happily ever after. Meanwhile, black kids will remain glued to the ghetto.

But things are beginning to change, and the pressure is finally getting to the rappers. Snoop Doggy Dogg, a very popular gangsta rapper, said on an MTV special that he looked forward to sitting down and talking to one of the most outspoken critics of the style, the Rev. Calvin O. Butts, pastor of New York's Abyssinian Baptist Church. Rap star Dogg has indicated he would be willing to tone down his lyrics, that rappers would be willing to listen to leaders who will lead. Bushwick Bill did apologize to the NABJ audience in Houston last year. Political leaders are bringing pressure on the performers and record company owners and radio stations. Some stations have stopped airing gangsta rap—a few black stations never did. And the majority of blacks, I am convinced, disagree with glorifying the rough lifestyle some gangsta rappers not only sing about but lead, including the flashing of guns, abuse of women and other antisocial behavior.

The courts will resolve the innocence or guilt in criminal charges several rappers are facing. But the public has already made certain judgments. Gangsta rap may have run its course as an expression of black youth and culture. The novelty seems to have worn off. There are those who feel that rap will make a lasting impression, much as the music of my youth, doo-wop, did. And they may be right. But positions are softening. On the MTV special, Dr. Dre, another popular and influential rapper, admitted that his motivation is strictly money: "I'm no gangsta," he said. "I'm here to make money." And some female groups—Queen Latifah and Salt 'n' Pepa, for example—are countering the macho men and urging women to demand respect. In the area of comedy, meanwhile, the depiction of blacks on many of the shows on television is a real throwback to an objectionable past era, but public pressure—and not assaults on the First Amendment—will most likely temper them.

Finally, some record companies are getting the message. Elektra rejected cover art for a new album by the group KMD that featured a white man in blackface being lynched. At the same time, though, there is growing (and legitimate, I suppose) debate about whether we are past the point of rejecting the likes of Amos 'n' Andy. Margo Jefferson wrote recently in the *New York Times* that she would not object if "Amos 'n' Andy" went back on the air. I don't think it is time yet—the country isn't ready. But we may be ready to debate the issue. As Mel Watkins notes, it certainly *is* time to give black comedy and other expressions their due. In that regard, by forcing the debate on the content and impact of black popular culture, gangsta rap may have been the wake-up call and opened up something that may be good.

The overriding concern for blacks in such a debate, though, will remain how it plays with whites. Blacks are still very sensitive on the topic— white racism is still too much alive and well in 1994 for blacks to ignore it, or to ease their vigilance in the face of it. Has America really reached the stage that black and white colleagues can stand around the water cooler and swap Amos 'n' Andy stories from last night's show? Sadly, my answer is, still, a resounding "no."

Paul Delaney, a former editor and reporter for the New York Times, *is chairman of the Department of Journalism at the University of Alabama.*

12

Racial Naming

Everette E. Dennis

*"My grandfather was colored, my father was a
Negro, and I am black."*

—Henry Louis Gates Jr.,
in his undergraduate application to Yale in 1969

The tortured history of racial, religious and ethnic name-calling in America makes clear the pain and pleasure associated with racial and ethnic monikers. Some names and descriptive terms do great damage to self- and group esteem, while others evoke identity and pride. For generations, civil convention has ruled that denigrating or insulting terms are out of line in written or spoken context. For the media, the exception has been direct quotes from conversations and incidents where a source's exact words are crucial to understanding. After all, a dispute ignited by a racial slur has little meaning if it is masked by a polite euphemism. Descriptors such as "racial epithet" or "barnyard vulgarity" simply lack the graphic force of cruel attacks like "nigger," "kike," "spic" or "wop."

At the same time, however, such street talk as "snapping," once called "the dozens"—in which members of the same racial group, in this instance African Americans, trade insults within their own ranks—can get confused in popular culture. In recent years, leaders such as the Rev. Calvin O. Butts of New York's Abyssinian Baptist Church and others have expressed concern about the increasingly common use of terms like "nigger," "ho" and "bitch" in rap music and popular music videos and films. When such banter intended for an "understanding" audience within the black community gets wider dissemination, it unintentionally ignites furor, angering parents of many ethnic and social backgrounds who implore their children to avoid such terms and use the language of tolerance and respect, rather than that of racism or sexism, of ethnic or religious hatred.

For the news media, dealing with such changing contours of language has proved difficult, because there are no easy indicators for the passage of particular terms into popular use so that they become racial or ethnic *lingua franca*. For example, when "African American" won the approval of some (though by no means all) black opinion leaders in the 1980s, a national poll suggested that most members of that racial group still preferred "black." Columnist Carl Rowan recounts a conversation with the Rev. Jesse Jackson, who urged adoption of "African American." Rowan had a succinct response: "To a black man who needs a job," he said, "it doesn't matter *what* they call him, just so long as they *call* him." The emphasis and energy of the black community should be on "real progress," not simply words, he said, especially when a neutral to positive term was being scrapped. "Since when," he asked, "did 'black' become so undesirable?" Change, though, seemed generational and inevitable, and the media began using both "black" and "African American" interchangeably.

The politics and practice of names and naming can be disorienting. For example, older Americans recall a time when "Negro" was the respectful and polite form, superseding "colored," which itself was once apparently acceptable as well. "Black," used both as a noun and as an adjective, was once thought to be denigrating but gained currency in the 1960s when the slogan "black is beautiful" was used by civil rights leaders and workers. More recently (and curiously), the catchall category "people of color" has received some acceptance, in part to avoid "minority" and "nonwhite," both of which were criticized as belittling to people who preferred not to be defined only in relation to whites, as either not majority or not white. Used by members of one racial group to describe groups with whom they feel affinity, such as African Americans and Latinos, it is rare that an individual prefers to call him or herself individually "a person of color." Typically, a more specific ethnic or racial identification is preferred over this generic catchall. The "people of color" phrase is potentially patronizing when used by members of the white race, itself a multicultural polyglot, to describe everybody other than themselves. Some students of language argue that the term is pretentious and ungrammatical. "You wouldn't ask anyone to pass you some 'paper of color,' would you?" asks one critic. The backlash acronym APOC, for "Almost a Person of Color," attaches to the sanctimonious individuals who behave as though they are part of a racial or ethnic group other than their own. Left unanswered is how to describe a person who hails from the Indian subcontinent? These people are Caucasians, but they are not white. Are they "people of color," too? Who decides?

Even more perplexing is the historic and continued use of the term "colored" by the respected National Association for the Advancement of Colored People. That's an official, legal name, of course, of an organization that no doubt has many members who prefer to be called "black" or "African American," probably not "colored" but possibly "people of color." Historian Henry Louis Gates Jr. puts the term in play again in his memoir, *Colored People,* published in 1994. In a letter to his daughters, he writes: "In your lifetimes, I suspect, you will go from being African Americans to 'people of color' to being, once again, 'colored people.'...I don't mind any of the names myself. But I have to confess that I like 'colored' best, maybe because when I hear the word, I hear in it my mother's voice and the sepia tones of my childhood." For some reason, the term "Afro-American," still used by scholars who study African-American culture and history, never really caught on with the mainstream media or the public.

In all of the designators, there are gross assumptions that hundreds of ethnic, cultural, language and racial groups can be easily categorized by skin tones. Brown, yellow, black and red have been used both in neutral and in negative fashion over the years. Especially stark is the division of America into white and nonwhite categories.

Native Americans, who, because of a navigational mistake by Christopher Columbus, were historically called Indians, often prefer their tribal identification (Navajo, Apache, Sioux, etc.). Many Native Americans took issue in the 1980s and 1990s with sports teams' use of nicknames like "redskins," "redmen," "braves" and "chiefs," arguing that sports mascots and team names were usually either animals or war-oriented, references constituting racism. (This is not completely the case, since Trojans and Vikings, for example, are human.) When the Atlanta Braves made it to the 1992 World Series, team owner Ted Turner and his wife, Jane Fonda, became the focal point of both TV coverage and angry Native American groups as they led fans in Atlanta stadium in "the Chop," which features foam-rubber tomahawks that symbolically behead Braves' opponents.

The *Oregonian* of Portland was among the first newspapers to refuse to use names that Native American groups decried, even though these were the established and legal names of the teams. Pending official name changes, the Washington Redskins simply became, to the *Oregonian*'s editors, Washington's professional football team. A few other papers respecting the wishes of Native Americans followed suit. Tim McGuire, editor of the Minneapolis *Star Tribune,* explained, "I doubt 'Fighting Irish' offends Irish folk like 'Redskins' affects Indians." Still, the acknowledged rule of thumb—to respect the preferences of African Americans and other groups—has not generally been extended to Native Americans.

The name wars continue in the Hispanic or Latino communities, which, like African Americans and Native Americans, hail from different countries, cultures and backgrounds. When the chiefs of state of all Spanish and Portuguese-speaking nations assemble, the occasion is called the "Ibero-American" summit, but that geographic moniker has not gained much currency. Many who prefer to call themselves "Latino," tracing their origins to Latin America or the Caribbean, say the term "Hispanic" was invented by immigration officials who wanted to differentiate new arrivals from Spain from those coming from Mexico and Latin America. Ellis Island officialdom around the turn of the century did the same thing to Italians, who came to America with little national identity, considering themselves natives of Venice, Naples, Sicily or Rome, but usually not Italians (united Italy, after all, dated only from the 1860s). One scholar traces the use of "Latino" to Texas in the 1930s, where it was used to repel prejudice against Mexicans and Mexican Americans. While some critics maintain that "Hispanic" is patently racist, it is argued that no one forces the Congressional Hispanic Caucus or the National Association of Hispanic Journalists to use it, which they do for good political reasons. Still, studies show that few persons under the Hispanic rubric accept the term and just a fraction use it. Some Mexican Americans in Southern California prefer the term "Chicano." Any assumption of Hispanic solidarity is quickly dispelled when one mentions the Cuban-American community, mostly based in Miami and ideologically separated from many other Americans who share a Spanish-language heritage.

Asian Americans have been less vocal about names and naming, but are no less passionate and not without legitimate grievances. From the

19th century forward, Chinese, Japanese and other ethnic Asians have faced slurs and virulent prejudice and discrimination. The term "Oriental," once quite common, has generally been replaced by "Asian American" or more specifically national designations—"Japanese-American," "Chinese-American," "Thai-American" and so on. "Oriental" is definitely out, regarded as racist by some newspaper stylebooks. Still, it is commonly used in Asia where, for example, the *Oriental Daily News,* a Cantonese-language newspaper in Hong Kong, seems oblivious to American ideas on this matter.

To the extent that the language of race is an instrument of intolerance, discrimination and even race hatred, attention to it is essential for the news media. Newspeople do play a profoundly important legitimizing and popularizing role as they debate names and terms. More often than not, they have followed, rather than led, public opinion regarding new designations for race and ethnicity. Two exceptions were racially sensitive stylebooks developed at the University of Missouri journalism school and the *Los Angeles Times*. Although well-meaning, they sometimes engaged in overkill in their politically correct sensitivity, for example objecting to the term "Dutch treat" as possibly offensive to residents of the Netherlands, who, as far as I know, never raised a fuss about this term. Essentially, while mostly avoiding labels that actually or potentially denigrate individuals or groups, the press is a prisoner of popular usage. To begin to call Latinos or Hispanics "Ibero-Americans" tomorrow would most likely confuse readers and viewers.

In the 1960s, some people argued that the media should be color-blind and not mention race at all unless it was particularly relevant to a story. By the 1990s, members of racial and ethnic groups most often want and expect direct identification and consider color-blind coverage paternalistic. Yet controversies remain as the media try to reconcile the preferences of people being described with terms that communicate accurately and with sensitivity. The continuing debate is marked both by seriousness as it attempts to promote tolerance and curb prejudice, and by some occasional silliness, too. One casualty of all this is humor, especially the humor of a given ethnic group, which may translate poorly and be badly misunderstood by the general audience.

To the extent that nit-picking over language interferes with coverage of vital racial and ethnic issues and problems, this debate, prolonged excessively, may be counterproductive. Nonetheless, conflict over language still intrigues, perplexes and maddens. And if this is a problem in the United States, consider the plight of countries with even more racial, ethnic, linguistic and other cultural differences than we have.

Everette E. Dennis is executive director of The International Consortium of Universities and senior vice president of The Freedom Forum. He was founding director and founding editor of The Media Studies Center at Columbia University and of the Media Studies Journal.

IV

A Media Industry Status Report

13

On-Ramps to the Information Superhighway

Adam Clayton Powell III

A simple exercise, for your consideration: Open a few of the new periodicals covering interactive media, say *Broadcasting*'s new Telemedia Week section, or the Interactive department of *Advertising Age.*

Then clip recent news articles on the progress of the on-line information and entertainment industry from mass-circulation magazines ranging from *Newsweek* to *Business Week.*

Now examine the latest reports on multimedia in daily newspapers ranging from the *New York Times* to *USA Today.* Finally, pick up the major computer magazines, from *MacWorld* to *PC.* Throw in *Wired,* too.

Now line them all up on a table. Arrange them in any order you want. Look at the photographs in each article. Look at the photographs in the advertisements. What do you see? It's a high-tech world populated entirely by whites.

Granted, this is highly anecdotal. Not scientifically rigorous. Too small a sample size. And there are exceptions: one African American in a group shot for IBM, another in a group shot for Apple, a few Asian Americans—or Asians in stories about looming competition from Japan or India.

Future archaeologists, studying the documentary record of the present, would have reason to conclude that people of color were bypassed by the information superhighway. Maybe it just passed *over* black and Latino communities, much as Manhattan's West Side Highway passes overhead on its way through Harlem neighborhoods. How accurate is this picture? Are the new information technologies created almost entirely by whites for almost entirely white audiences and consumers? If so, what does this mean?

The new media are still in their infancy, or perhaps they are toddling. They still have not reached the point of explosive growth, of mass acceptance by a mass audience. That means they are still heavily influenced by the pioneers, just as radio was in the early days of Marconi and Bell. And if information superhighway hobbyists are those who can combine expertise with access to business skills and capital, they are even less likely to be people of color. Further, information superhighway lobbyists are disproportionately white; if you select from among them those who are both knowledgeable and able to raise the kind of money it takes to start companies with a stake in the electronic future, you have a subgroup that is even *less* diverse.

"There are relatively few people of color involved in new media," acknowledges Stan Thomas, president and CEO of Time Warner's new interactive Sega Channel. "It is very technically oriented. In the end, the industry takes people who went to MIT and Cal Tech." Thomas, one of the very few minority senior executives in emerging technologies, worries that the dominance of "techies" from overwhelmingly white technical ranks can lead to insensitivities in delivery and packaging of content on the information superhighway, just as it once did in other media.

To appreciate the scope of some of these insensitivities, remember those advertisements in the computer and multimedia magazines. Consider how many other consumer industries would feature all-white marketing campaigns in the mid-1990s.

The government's policy-making apparatus also reflects this demographic bias, offering little reassurance to those concerned that minorities might be left out of policy planning for the new technologies, exacerbating the gap between information haves and have-nots. Certainly, the new White House Advisory Council on the National Information Infrastructure is less than universally inclusive.

"When [the NII Council] was first announced, there were several African Americans and several women, but no Hispanics" on it, recalls Eduardo Gomez, president and general manager of KABQ Radio in Albuquerque and himself a new addition to the Council. "Even now, the Hispanic community and Hispanic broadcasters are underrepresented. It means one person [Gomez himself] is going to have his hands full trying to represent all of these constituencies."

Industry groups and government policy-makers may mirror today's consumers of new media: Current data indicate those new media consumers also are disproportionately white and male. Limited to those with personal computers, multimedia platforms and CD-ROM drives, the customer base is an elite fragment of the U.S. population. Most Internet connections are at offices and laboratories, not in the home, further limiting the kind of people who have access to it.

This will change, and quickly, as computers become inexpensive home appliances (which we may still call television sets), linked to powerful central file servers by wires (which we may still call cable television, or telephone wires). But for the moment, despite its expense and difficulty of use, the hobbyists' hardware still rules, and so do the techies. And, in turn, according to those surveyed for this article, that means industry meetings, panels and conferences rarely feature, or are attended by, people of color.

"Production managers and techies are the types who attend industry meetings," observes Susan Bokern, associate director of Gannett New Business. "I can say, having gone to a lot of those meetings, that you don't see a lot of blacks, although you do see some Asians. And this is an indication of who took these subjects in schools. It's not the liberal arts majors."

Bokern believes more women and minorities will eventually be drawn to new technologies, attracted by broader marketing and enabled by learning computer skills in elementary schools. And MIT and Cal Tech are admitting many more minority students and women than a generation ago.

Gomez wants to encourage more rapid progress on college campuses. One of his first priorities was to persuade the NII Advisory Council to begin a study comparing predominantly white universities to historically black colleges and colleges in the Hispanic Association of Colleges and Universities. Gomez wants to see the extent of the differences in wired and unwired networks on white and nonwhite college campuses, and he is insisting the Council design a program to draw interns for new media from predominantly black and Latino campuses.

But until this educated base trickles up, Bokern fears techies' dominance will continue to exert a profound impact on both the form and content of the new media, even as their influence starts to wane.

"Techies developed new media for themselves," she says. "New technology used to be just a techie area, but now it has broadened out to editors and marketing people. The subject matter is becoming more mainstream."

This represents a significant shift in outlook. Consider parallels in another new mass market medium that reaches far more Americans than the Internet—cable television. In less than two decades, cable evolved from a service tool to bring television to viewers not reached by over-the-air signals to a huge program-distribution network reaching most of the American people.

From the early days of cable as a mass medium, the industry provided opportunities for minorities that were not available in the older video medium of broadcasting. Thus, we saw Bernard Shaw on CNN long before Bryant Gumbel hosted NBC's "Today" show and Connie Chung anchored the "CBS Evening News." In music, after initially declining to feature minority artists, MTV discovered it could prosper by putting black musicians in heavy rotation, first with Michael Jackson in the 1980s and then with an assortment of rappers in the 1990s. And Robert Johnson, founder of Black Entertainment Television, grabbed the opportunity of the new medium to become one of the wealthiest minority businessmen in the nation's history.

It took many years of work in the cable industry before Stan Thomas was appointed to run the Sega Channel. Even so, Thomas believes cable television's opportunities for people of color may have been an aberration in the media.

"Cable was something of an exception," Thomas says, not so much in terms of the hardware (or systems—techie—area), but on the program (or software) side.

"When I was sitting down to negotiate with cable [hardware] companies," Thomas recalls, "it was infrequent that anyone else in the room with me was a person of color."

As a result, the new media could have offered minority programmers and entrepreneurs a vast array of new opportunities. But they didn't or, at least, haven't so far: Gomez points out that minority-owned broadcast companies rarely are found at the desirable positions on the dial.

"Spanish-language broadcasters have traditionally been relegated to the worst frequencies, at the upper end of the AM dial," points out Gomez, who is vice president of the American Hispanic-Owned Radio Association. "AM stations are going off the air in city after city. As new technologies develop, we have to make an effort to make certain we are there for the first opportunities. This time, we want to get in on the ground floor."

But those who look to government intervention and subsidies may not always find the result they are seeking. Consider another major medium created in the past generation, delivered by broadcast radio and television: public broadcasting.

Created by regulatory action and funded largely by a billion-dollar federal appropriation, big-budget public television and radio today appears to viewers and listeners as devoid of minorities as the new information technologies. The Public Broadcasting Service is the only broadcast network without a single prime-time program hosted by or featuring any minorities (and, except for Diana Rigg, no PBS hosts are women). And unlike its commercial radio counterparts, National Public Radio has no minority anchors on any of its morning or afternoon news programs, seven days a week, reversing gains made in the 1980s. If Bill Clinton, who promised an administration that "looked like America," had named a cabinet that looked like public broadcasting, he would have been justifiably excoriated—perhaps most loudly on public TV and radio.

There are exceptions, small community-service stations struggling along on minuscule funding. But with the bulk of federal funds earmarked for wealthy institutions, the perverse policy result is that taxes from Latino and African-American and Asian and Native American families go to pay for a system of affluent white producers serving affluent white audiences.

Now coming under the same political and bureaucratic forces that shaped public broadcasting, the new information technologies could also be forced to adopt public broadcasting's complexion. Many optimists say this will not happen, looking to older print and broadcast traditions as instruments for broadening the diversity of the newcomers.

"The good news," says Sega's Stan Thomas, "is that interactive media are the results of other media—movies, games, information services, television."

This may naturally invite uncomfortable questions of how well the older media have included all of the communities they cover, and whose dollars they covet. If the optimistic future of the demographics of new media is reflected in the face of newspapers, as some suggest, one must confront newspapers' less-than-successful record of hiring and promoting, and covering and marketing to, minorities.

In the weeks and months ahead, the federal policy apparatus will be active on several fronts, at the White House, in Congress and at various federal agencies, designing the regulations that will govern and shape the new media and the new information technologies.

At the Federal Communications Commission, Rutgers Professor Jorge Schement has been working on a report on universal service for the Commission's chairman. Schement plans to complete the report over the summer and deliver it to FCC Chairman Reed Hundt in the fall, with Commission action possible this winter. Watch for congressional hearings on a similar timetable.

Lawmakers and regulators will struggle with questions of fairness and equity, and of access for non-mainstream consumers, many of whom are racial minorities. And much of the discussion will focus not on economics but on who we Americans are and where we fit in the global village of a brave new electronic world.

"The national information infrastructure is going to extend outside of the United States," Gomez notes, "and it must be multilingual. For every English speaker in this hemisphere, there are two who speak Spanish." Indeed, it has been estimated that the United States soon will be the largest Spanish-speaking nation on earth.

A key question will center on the use of cross-subsidies, government grants, or a mix of both. This past spring, cable entrepreneur Ted Turner proposed a similar concept, suggesting payments by "cable stamps," the electronic equivalent of food stamps.

That may seem self-serving, since it would enable many new viewers to watch Turner's programs, including CNN and offerings on the Turner Broadcasting System, but a variation on that plan may yet become reality, at least as a limited test: On Capitol Hill, some Democratic Party leaders are considering a program that would provide information subsidies for families that cannot otherwise afford connections to high-capacity lines from cable television or telephone companies.

If the cable and telephone companies were to offer volume discounts for "lifeline" service, to reduce the cost to, say, $10 a month for access to the information highway, the subsidy would total perhaps $120 per year per household. To cover the poorest 5 percent of American households with total subsidies would cost less than $500 million a year, considerably less than the federal contribution to the operating and capital budgets of public television and radio stations.

Such lifeline cable TV service would offer access to the major basic program services—CNN for news, Nickelodeon for children, Discovery for documentaries, A&E for history and drama and, for public affairs, C-SPAN 1, 2 and 3. And a threshold lifeline service might easily also offer some level of interactivity for those who connect devices ranging from video games to computers. This vision raises the issue of whether computer terminals also should be subsidized. Argument in favor: Until relatively recently, a telephone line came with a terminal (the telephone). Argument against: We already have achieved universal video service, with households at all income levels purchasing their terminals (television sets).

But in an era of ever-tightening spending caps, Congress might have difficulty finding a spare half a billion dollars or so for such a subsidy to the private cable industry. Or maybe not: Some Democrats already have been looking closely at the Corporation for Public Broadcasting subsidy as a source of funds to extend universal service to America's poor. After all, reasoned one key Democrat (considered a friend of public broadcasting), if poor families had access to Nickelodeon, A&E, CNN and C-SPAN, those networks would provide the same services now seen on PBS, and then some.

And, so the scenario goes, PBS favorites would migrate to the other channels: The National Geographic Society's program already has returned to commercial television. Nickelodeon would be ecstatic at the thought of scheduling "Sesame Street," even without commercials. "Masterpiece Theater" and "Mystery" might easily go to A&E, which already has the rights to BBC productions. And wouldn't CNN snap up MacNeil and Lehrer as eagerly as it signed their former contributor, Judy Woodruff?

As a bonus in such a scheme, all of those families connected to the telephone and cable program services would also be connected to the information superhighway. And that, in turn, would motivate information providers to develop more services, just as broadcast television evolved similarly when their audiences grew and broadened. It is a "field of dreams" strategy in reverse—If you come, they will build it.

As in the early years of cable television, these next few years of the new information technologies will offer extraordinary opportunities for minority entrepreneurs and managers who can design and sell services for markets overlooked by the white "techie" pioneers. But that window of opportunity may last only until the new media begin to mature, when the older media industries extend their corporate cultures, and their corporate hiring and promotion practices, to tame the new media frontier. The window, for racial minority communities, may well be very small.

On the one extreme, the new media could produce the next Bob Johnson or Connie Chung. On the other, the information superhighway could produce an alabaster facade, like public broadcasting. Somewhere in between is a path not dissimilar to today's universal medium, broadcast television.

The difference will be in the details, in subtle shifts of policy and market regulation, to permit and encourage the broad fluidity of opportunity and access, or to exclude new drivers from merging onto the information highway.

And in the end, it is all a business, like any other. "I don't know if interactive media are any worse than any other media, or any other discipline," observes Thomas. "They just reflect the reality of the American business experience." While the new information technologies that will make up the interactive future represent—like other media developments that came before them—an opportunity to make America's media system as diverse as its "melting pot" population, the stern realities of America's past business experience mitigate against universality. Traffic on the information superhighway could be truly representative, but past experience makes that eventuality a bad bet.

Adam Clayton Powell III, who has worked in cable and both commercial and public television and radio, is vice president of technology at The Freedom Forum.

14

Newspapers' Quest for Racial Candor

Sig Gissler

Race—it is America's rawest nerve and most enduring dilemma. From birth to death, race is with us, defining, dividing, distorting. The strained relationship is discussed almost obsessively, if not directly then indirectly, through code words, masked references, rolls of the eye. In New York City recently, I received a dollar bill in change. Someone had printed two words in red ink under George Washington's portrait: "Slave Owner."

Race particularly troubles urban America—our centers of business, industry, education, music, art and culture where the nation's destiny in the 21st century will play out. Indeed, racial mistrust is likely to grow in significance as America's minority population swells, new racial and ethnic rivalries emerge, and the economy continues to restructure, with jagged results.

Meanwhile, let none mistake the news media's vital role. Journalism helps shape how racially diverse people think of each other and how public policy on race-related issues is formulated.

Yet, despite the importance of race and the deep public interest in it, the media's coverage tends to be fragmented, episodic, confused, misdirected and sometimes cowardly. When there's a chance for better understanding of black family life, for example, the media often are sensational or superficial. Present a chance for better coverage of race in urban politics—increasingly laced with conflicts between blacks and browns as well as between blacks and whites—and the media often respond with clichés and superficialities. When there's a chance for better perspective on "inner-city crime," the media often are mired in the lurid. Worst of all, when there's a chance for frankness on race-related problems (such as

AIDS or teen pregnancy) or racial tensions (such as white backlash in the workplace), the media often are cryptic, ambiguous or timid. In short, the media in America too regularly mangle their crucial mission as regards race.

Even so, there is hope. Last year, two newspapers—one in the South, the other in the North—plunged deeply and courageously into racial honesty. Their sometimes agonizing efforts were acclaimed. The *New Orleans Times-Picayune,* (circulation: 272,000 daily, 330,000 Sunday), led by a white editor and a white publisher, won the Society of Professional Journalists' annual Sigma Delta Chi award for public service. The *Akron Beacon Journal,* (159,000 daily, 229,000 Sunday), led by a white editor and a black publisher, won the 1994 Pulitzer Prize for public service.

The idea for the *Times-Picayune's* project arose after ex-Klu Klux Klansman David Duke won nearly 40 percent of Louisianans' votes in his 1991 bid for governor, dramatizing the omnipresent influence of race in Louisiana. Knight-Ridder's *Beacon Journal* decided to look at the issue of race in its hometown because of the jolting 1992 riots in Los Angeles and the approaching 30th anniversary of Martin Luther King Jr.'s "I Have a Dream" speech.

The projects reflect the brighter side of flawed media performance. Clearly, the media have progressed since the Kerner Commission in 1968 warned that America was becoming two societies, one black, one white: separate and unequal. For example, despite excessive foot-dragging, both editors and broadcasters have slowly improved racial coverage by diversifying staff, leadership and content.

Sometimes, in fact, the journalism is superb. In 1992, the *Los Angeles Times'* riot coverage was exemplary. In 1993, the Chicago Tribune documented the murder of every youngster in its metropolitan area, giving value to all young lives. The *New York Times* explored urban America's "Children of the Shadows." The *Cleveland Plain Dealer* looked at "Kids Without Marriage" (both white and black children). *Newsweek,* which has a tradition of bold race reporting, did a candid cover story on the imperiled black family.

At times, television news, too, takes racial coverage well beyond blood, bullets and sound bites. In 1989, not long after CBS fired Jimmy (the Greek) Snyder for his remarks about "breeding" black athletes, NBC's Tom Brokaw did a gutsy special report on "Black Athletes: Fact and Fiction." Recently, CBS's "48 Hours" aired an insightful report on interracial love. And this year, Deborah Weiner, a Baltimore TV reporter, won a duPont award for crime coverage that included a sensitive look at forgotten survivors of violence, many of them minorities.

However, because of their exceptional breadth, depth and candor on questions of race in their communities, the New Orleans and Akron projects deserve closer inspection. Here's what was done and what lessons might be learned.

In New Orleans, "It was a bitch," Jim Amoss says with a chuckle. "But I would never undo it. It was so valuable."

Thoughtful, low-key, Amoss has been editor of the *Times-Picayune* since 1990. At the end of a long day, he was talking about his paper's blunt inquiry into New Orleans' 300-year-old struggle with race.

Both an ordeal and a high accomplishment for the newspaper, the project was entitled "Together Apart: The Myth of Race," appearing in installments between May and November of 1993. For the project team, initially composed of about 18 members, the venture began in disarray and distrust. Before even an outline could be prepared, there were weeks of often emotional meetings, initially with staff group therapy, aided by an outside consultant (sample question: Can a white person not be a racist?).

Looking back, Keith Woods, a black journalist who pushed the project as city editor and who now is a columnist and editorial writer, says he lost white friends and suffered some of the deepest pain in his life in the process. While proud of the project, he says, "As a human being, I don't want to do that again."

Kristin Gilger, a white editor from the Midwest who supervised the project, recalls the team's wobbly start. The first meeting was called to brainstorm, a process that quickly collapsed. "We couldn't agree on anything," she says. "Not even what racism is."

Gilger, now managing editor at the Salem (Ore.) *Statesman Journal,* recalls the group's reaction when a black staff member said any honest project on race must deal with slavery: "White people in the room rolled their eyes and said, 'Jesus Christ, why do we have to talk about slavery? It happened 300 years ago.'"

Ultimately, the project did address slavery, which had been a flourishing business in old New Orleans. In fact, the paper asserted that the city's troubled race relations are "rooted" in a history of white people enslaving black people and that New Orleanians "have not completely broken free of that history." In the *Times-Picayune*'s stories, slavery did not just happen; it was imposed. "We didn't use the passive voice," Amoss says. "White people were actors—which upsets people. They find it very hard to buy into."

With that moral tone, the project explored relations between blacks and whites on a wide range of issues—housing, education and employment to religion and interracial marriage. Along the way, the paper examined a bundle of racial myths. A story on athletics was headed, "White people can jump. Black people can lead."

Early in the project, the paper also confessed its own sins, which ranged from editorial support of white supremacy in bygone years to seriously distorted coverage of black people in recent years. For example, until August 1990, the 156-year-old newspaper published separate pages for black and white debutantes. White debs got a Sunday section to themselves, while black debs were shown over several days in regular issues without the biographies that white debs received.

Amoss, who wants his paper to reflect the region's culture and diversity, found the confessions "excruciating," partly because "we were talking not just about our distant selves but our recent selves when most of us were participants."

The *Times-Picayune*'s publisher, Ashton Phelps Jr., was aware of everything that went into the paper and, in Amoss's view, was "very courageous." He would ask questions, usually about balance, but never ordered a retreat, Amoss says.

The forbearance was especially notable because of the project's sharp edge. Some white readers were turned off. About 1,000 canceled subscriptions (and perhaps half still have not returned). However, the editors believe that most readers stuck with the series.

In fact, the *Times-Picayune* solicited and received strong, sustained reader reaction, pro and con. To the editors' surprise, more than 6,500 readers responded with messages on a special recorded telephone line. "We found an incredible interest," Gilger says. The paper eventually ran 58 pages of often candid comments, some signed, some not. The fascinating pages had the vitality of talk radio without its worst vices.

In northeast Ohio, the *Akron Beacon Journal*'s venture into racial frankness was calmly entitled "A Question of Color." Appearing in five chunky installments over 11 months, the series did not delve into racial history or focus on fault. Yet, in its own way, it was striking.

Special projects editor Bob Paynter, who is white, described how his team approached its task: "We're going to take a look at race and political correctness be damned. We're going to explore race in the round." So, using survey research, focus groups and database analysis to augment old-fashioned investigation, the paper explored the stark impact of skin color on community life, letting the facts largely speak for themselves.

As the project gained momentum, the *Beacon Journal,* under the banner "Coming Together," began explicitly to encourage racial bridge-building among groups and ordinary individuals. It was an unorthodox step for a newspaper, given the journalistic ethos of noninvolvement in civic ventures. It also helped win Akron the Pulitzer Prize.

How did the project team fare emotionally? "Very smoothly sometimes, very rocky other times," says Dale Allen, the *Beacon Journal*'s editor since 1986. The team's initial meetings were similar to those at the *Times-Picayune,* but apparently with less prolonged agony.

"We locked black and white team members in a room for a day to brainstorm," recalls Paynter, the special projects editor. "At times it became like an encounter group. People told personal stories. There was some crying." It took several weeks to get the project rolling. Allen applauds the process: "Our goal was to get at the truth. And the truth hurts."

Akron publisher John Dotson, one of the few black chief executives in the newspaper business, took a supportive interest in the project. Once, he raised what Paynter calls a helpful prepublication question about a story on black crime that neglected to deal with crimes committed by whites (a black copy editor raised similar concerns). After discussion, Paynter amended the piece, making it "more informative."

Truth-telling certainly marked the published stories. As the project moved from topic to topic, the paper made extensive use of citizen focus groups. At first, whites and blacks met in racially separate sessions. Midway through the project, the groups merged and talked together. Often the remarks in the initial session were pointed, even raw, the sort seldom heard in polite discourse. After the groups melded, that kind of candor did not disappear, but it diminished.

Reporters covered the focus groups and wrote long, quote-packed stories. Although focus group participants were guaranteed anonymity, some agreed to let the paper use their names and pictures, strengthening the stories' authenticity. It took courage. Many participants declined. In the end, Akron—and its newspaper—learned a lot about black-white divisions, and about the opportunity for finding common ground.

In its final installment, the project turned a spotlight on the *Beacon Journal* itself. Two groups of black and white staffers (not project team members) met separately with focus group leaders to assess the paper's coverage of crime, perhaps the most difficult of race-related issues for journalists. The differences were significant. For example, some black staffers felt the paper overplayed black crime, while some white staffers felt black-on-white crime was muffled. When the two groups merged, candor receded.

The published story on the sessions showed that, much like the public, black and white journalists can look at an issue and see divergent realities, as if watching different movies. Moreover, they find it hard to talk to each other about their perceptions.

Audience reaction to the project was strong. While some readers were irked ("I'm so sick of this poor black stuff," wrote one woman), the affirmative response was remarkable. In a metropolitan area of 500,000, no fewer than 22,000 persons sent in coupons pledging to help improve race relations. Meanwhile, more than 140 organizations, representing more than 10,000 members, have volunteered to promote racial understanding. The newspaper serves as a "catalyst," says Allen, but leaves the agenda to the groups. Allen acknowledges that the newspaper's activism has critics, even inside his newsroom. His solution to concerns about maintaining sufficient journalistic independence: "We told the groups that we'll cover you if you make news, and it might be good or it might be bad."

In certain respects, these two projects differ. The *Times-Picayune* was more sweeping and judgmental in its effort. The *Beacon Journal* was more focused, with an activist twist. Yet both projects speak volumes about journalism and race.

• They challenge the notion that Americans are "tired" of reading and hearing about race. Executed with honesty, integrity and imagination, even a long newspaper series that closely and critically examines issue of race can engage and hold an audience.

• These cases illustrate why newsrooms, both print and electronic, shy away from racial candor. Open coverage of such a threatening secret can upset the audience, raise anxiety, perhaps rip a staff apart. It's easier to cover racial stories in the conventional superficial manner and keep a lid on feelings. In newsrooms, race is usually discussed warily. Black reporters, for example, are often reluctant to speak up for fear of being tagged whiners. Meanwhile, white reporters bite their tongues for fear of being labeled racists, the most scalding epithet in the news business today. To their credit, both the New Orleans and Akron papers acted on the belief that honest dialogue, however initially painful and threatening, ultimately reduces fear, mistrust and anger.

• The New Orleans and Akron examples underline the importance of racial diversity in a newsroom's staff and leadership. The *Times-Picayune* staff is 14 percent minority; the *Beacon Journal*'s is 20 percent. All-white reporting teams would have missed important story angles, nuances, unconventional sources. The feelings of ordinary black citizens are especially important in all kinds of newspaper coverage. "Their perceptions are their realities," says Colette Jenkins, a black reporter at the *Beacon Journal* who interviewed black people for Akron's segment on education. In Louisiana, Amoss makes a similar point: "We don't realize how much our newspapers reflect one point of view—the white point of view."

• These cases demonstrate how the media can influence racial attitudes within communities and newsrooms. In New Orleans, the series became part of the city's consciousness. Many people used reprints to stimulate racial dialogue in schools, churches and elsewhere. "I think the series still works on people in ways they don't fully express," Amoss says. In Akron, the paper offered "a glimpse of hope," Allen says, by actively promoting racial understanding. He tells of a wealthy white woman who came to a newspaper-sponsored community meeting and, for the first time in her life, shook hands with a black person. In its next phase, the *Beacon Journal* is encouraging every reader to make an interracial friend, and publishing tips on how to do it.

As for the newsrooms themselves, where skepticism thrives, the results are mixed. Most deeply affected by the projects were the team members themselves. In both cities, journalists now feel greater ease in discussing race, of being able to raise questions without raising racial hackles. "We have a better vocabulary, says one reporter. Says another, "It takes practice, a lot of practice."

But the wider newsroom conversation about race often remains constrained, despite the newspapers' efforts. "We have the pervasive potential for a dialogue closer to honesty," says Woods, the black *Times-Picayune* reporter. "We also have potential for backsliding." Clearly, managing a multicultural newsroom requires constant, imaginative attention.

Nonetheless, both Amoss and Allen see progress. Thanks to the projects, newsroom sensitivity training, increased minority staffing and other steps, they believe their papers today deal more effectively with race in the newsroom and in the news columns. The challenge is to avoid the roller-coaster syndrome. When riots erupt in Los Angeles or the Rev. Jesse Jackson calls a national summit on black-on-black crime, media reporting reaches a peak of intensity, then quickly drops off. Excellence requires perseverance, telling the story of race, day in and day out, with consistency, context and fortitude.

Are journalists really racial cowards? After newsroom focus-group sessions in Akron, a white journalist anonymously noted, "We journalists, the very persons who want to find truth...by getting people to share with us what is in their hearts, proved to be more guarded in addressing crime and race relations in the newsroom than those who we decry for their lack of candor. Why? Because who knows better than a journalist the consequences of opening your heart and spilling your guts all over a newspaper page?"

Amoss comes at the cowardice question differently. "People are resistant to pain," he says. "To talk about race in America is to visit a very painful area. So people stay away from it." In avoiding pain, he says, newspapers are no different than their readers.

He's right. But every journalist, in print or on television, has a professional obligation to be more daring about race. The nation depends on it.

The riots that followed the Rodney King beating case in Los Angeles put race squarely back at the top of America's agenda and spurred media attention, from major analytical reports to increased minority hiring efforts. Today, Shelby Coffey, editor of the *Los Angeles Times,* keeps two rocks the size of California grapefruits on the coffee table in his office. They are mementos of that April night in 1992 when Los Angeles erupted, and a mob smashed ground-floor windows of his newspaper's downtown headquarters. It got dramatic. At one point, Coffey brandished a pair of scissors to drive back rioters from his newspaper lobby. For Coffey, and for the media, the rocks symbolize a basic truth about race: We'd better deal honestly with the truth of racial enmity in this country before it deals with us, perhaps by crashing through the office window.

Sig Gissler was editor of the Milwaukee Journal *and now is a professor in the Graduate School of Journalism at Columbia University.*

15

¡Ya Viene Atzlan! Latinos in U.S. Advertising

Lisa Peñaloza

In her book, *Borderlands/La Frontera,* Gloria Anzaldúa recasts the myth of *Atzlan* to the contemporary United States, a "land [that] was Mexican once, was Indian always, and is. And will be again." For Anzaldúa, *Atzlan* is as much a state of mind as a homeland where chicanos/chicanas finally get our due, having worked through a complex history of conquest and oppression to build a vibrant and versatile culture, a labor of love that we carry with humility and pride. Camelot it's not. The 21st century is to be the era of *la mestiza,* Anzaldúa writes, the mixed blood one who glides betwixt and between worlds, multiethnic and multiracial, gleaning aspects of many cultures into a whole new entity. Here, the "other" has been integrated into the self, and cultural homogeneity and purity are exposed as a futile veneer.

Anzaldúa is not alone in her invocation of the powerful myth. *Return to Atzlan* is the title of demographer Doug Massey's recent book on growth and change in the U.S. population. For the past decade, demographers have noted the growth rates of Latinos as five times that of the U.S. population as a whole and offered startling predictions as to the United States of the future, when Latinos are expected to surpass blacks as the largest racial minority group. Together, minorities currently comprise 24 percent of the U.S. population and are expected to exceed 30 percent by the year 2000. Already, "minorities" are the majority in major cities; in many metropolitan areas, this has been so for more than 10 years.

In the advertising world, representations of minorities have been a topic of interest that has waxed and waned since the civil rights movement. Terms such as "invisibility," "stereotypes" and "segregation" abound in this literature, and there is a growing sense that there are similar stakes at issue now. Debate often follows a black-white binary, as scholars lament the few minorities in ads in "mainstream" media, while criticizing ads in minority media for being "too white."

Yet, so much has changed in the last 20 years that to view minorities in advertising solely in terms of inclusions in "mainstream" media is to miss much of it. The growth rates for minority populations have proven to be a lucrative base for sustaining minority media and are changing the structure and character of the media and of advertising in general. Media conglomerates are developing the Latino market via partnerships and buyouts of previously independent media, resulting in an influx of new newspapers, inserts and magazines for Latinos.

Like the *mestiza,* advertisers are scrambling to make sense of a media environment that is no longer comprised of a singular mainstream culture (if indeed it ever was); today the mainstream consists of an amalgam of diverse subcultures. To understand the significance of minorities in advertising, we need to be more creative in thinking about what advertisements depicting minorities and whites mean to both minorities and whites, and in both mainstream and minority media together as each is locked into a powerful symbiotic relationship with its "other." Race/ethnicity has never been a "people of color" issue, although it is often treated as such. Dismissing ads in minority media as white perpetuates a white standard of reading images that are much more ambiguous when grounded in more than one cultural system.

During the civil rights movement, groups such as the Mexican American Legal Defense Fund and the National Association for the Advancement of Colored People pressured firms to represent Latinos and blacks more positively in their ads. Underlying this activism was the recognition that advertising and market targeting were important means of public visibility and legitimation in our society. These organizations used advertising depictions to raise public consciousness as to the subtle yet pervasive effects of negative stereotypes, highlighting the ways advertising images both draw from and reproduce limited notions of minorities.

Partly the result of gains of the social movements, but increasingly the result of recognition of minorities' market potential, progress has been noted in the representation of minorities in "mainstream" advertising. By 1980, only 14 percent of blacks in advertisements were depicted in low-skilled jobs, with 89 percent shown in equal-status capacities to that of whites, researchers Samuel Gaertner and John Davidio found in the mid-1980s. Frito-Lay retired the Frito Bandito, Aunt Jemima got a new look, and Sambo's went out of business. Minorities now appear in advertisements for automobiles, computers, clothing, liquor and cigarettes, as well as in corporate image advertising; yet most of these ads are found in minority media.

Here lies the dilemma: Latinos are invisible in general-interest media, yet appear in rich luxurious images in Latino media. According to a recent study, *Invisible People,* sponsored by the Department of Consumer Affairs of New York City, few Latinos were found in general-interest magazines, and those who did appear were featured stereotypically as hired help, disadvantaged children or as a tokenistic part of a group in corporate message ads.

Given so few placements of minorities in these media, companies that do include minorities in their advertising are wide open to charges of tokenism. But this is only partially the result of context. Social movements tend to perpetuate a type of essentialism by privileging the interests of their members in efforts to further their causes. Within these movements and the subcultures and consciousness they foster, it is not enough to be included as one of several kinds of people. In a similar vein, Latino media may be seen to provide an alternative reality that represents Latinos almost exclusively.

Corporate message advertisements, while arguably done with the best of intentions, stem from a patronizing model of disadvantaged people of color being saved by the great white people and their companies. An Arco ad, which ran in *Hispanic* in May 1994, offers an example of this conflict, representing Arco as gracious benefactor of the Latino community. When I see ads like these, I think, "If only the community had received the money the businesses spent on these campaigns," and wonder how many people like to think of themselves as having been helped.

The most serious limitation of studies of minorities in general-interest media, however, is that they render minorities even more invisible by ignoring minority media. Yet there has been tremendous growth in these media and in advertising firms catering to these markets since their "discovery" in the mid 1980s and 1970s, for Latinos and blacks, respectively. I say "discovery" because, like the "new world," minority media existed long before this. In fact, there were over a hundred Spanish-language newspapers in the United States at the turn of the century. Latinos have historically turned to our media for information on our community, and these media have been supported for the most part by local and regional advertisers for a range of products and services.

Reaction to the Latino advertising boom has been mixed. Seeing Latinos in ads gives us a strong sense of validation. Latino media reflect our growing market power, estimated at 27 million people and $170 *billion* in annual spending. For companies interested in targeting Latino audiences, the numbers are found in these Spanish and English "specialty" newspapers and magazines. These media, together with ad agencies specializing in the Latino market, sell that market to advertisers with much hype and some truth. The Latino market has been dubbed the sleeping giant, with consumers described as brand-loyal and willing to pay extra for name brands.

Images of Latinos in ads in Latino media are both affirming and seductive—just as they are for whites and blacks. They are selected images that anticipate people's aspirations for beauty, success, power and material possessions. But it is incorrect to equate these images with whiteness, because this reserves these markers of success in our society to whites. Latinos have their own valid claim to middle-class success symbols as consumers of cars, insurance, perfume and even whiteness.

Yet the key question facing the Latino community is whether Latino media will continue to serve us—especially in the face of buyouts and takeovers. These media developed partly in response to Latino exclusion from other media and partly in response to the demands of the community, demands that were not addressed by other media. The concern with the "mainstreaming" of the Latino media is that it may downplay the hard political issues confronting Latino communities—e.g., our persistent socioeconomic gap with whites, our 50 percent high school dropout rate and the high incidence of teen pregnancy—out of fear of losing advertising dollars.

Yet this is not the concern that preoccupies most media scholars. They are more concerned that people of color are invisible in the general-interest media and that Latino and other "specialized" media preclude the possibility of a general media forum in our society, hence further separating the country.

New York City's Department of Consumer Affairs recently called on media and consumer products companies to voluntarily include more images of minorities in print advertising. The reasoning behind these calls was that it was economically dumb to ignore minority spending power of $400 billion annually. Yet while half of ad executives surveyed by *Advertising Age* felt that advertising had an influence on racial problems in America and agreed that there were too few minorities in print ads, none would sign the voluntary inclusion pledge. Advertising and media practitioners claimed it wasn't their job, that they merely followed advertisers' wishes. For their part, magazine publishers also said it wasn't their job to regulate race in their advertisers' ads.

But are the numbers really that sound? While $400 billion is no small sum, no single medium has access to the whole market. More critically, does it make sense that advertisers place ads in media where people of color are 10 percent to 20 percent of the total readership? Meanwhile, media and advertising firms specializing in the Latino market defy the ad slump of the past few years. Crayola has added a wider range of "flesh" colors to their boxes of crayons, doll companies now put brown skin and wider noses on some of their dolls, white women broaden their lips, and rap music is hot among white male American youth. Montgomery Ward has signed on Cristina as a celebrity endorser, and two Denver newspapers have added special sections for Latinos, as have other newspapers eager to capture new readers.

While there is reason to be concerned about increasing segmentation of American society, partly the result of market targeting, many welcome the affirmation and the democratizing impulse of minority-market targeting. Yet I wonder whether media critics' worries about social separation are not a subtle attempt to reposition white magazines at the center. The question of whether specialized media divide the country invokes a false nostalgia that we were once united. This is why critics don't raise concerns about separation when another general-interest magazine is born.

Separation strikes a deep chord in this society. Just as discrimination in social policy became intolerable in the "Great Society" ushered in by Presidents Kennedy and Johnson, separation of media audiences has been suspect. Yet it is hardly a coincidence that the rise of market segmentation came at roughly the same time as civil rights activism. Since the 1970s, the U.S. market has been in the process of becoming more specialized and more fragmented. Segmentation partially explains the backlash noted in the 1992 New York City follow-up study *Still Invisible,* which found fewer people of color in mainstream media today than 15 years ago. Advertisers increasingly are targeting minorities in minority media.

Minorities are not the only ones affected by market fragmentation, however. The legitimation that market targeting has brought to minorities has been accompanied by a qualification of whiteness such that white is no longer equal to the general interest and the mainstream. One of the early responses advertisers made to the charge that they were not showing people of color remains telling today. People of color weren't used because the magazines catered to white audiences.

In media studies, whiteness remains paradoxically everywhere and nowhere. White media and white people have shown a resistance to thinking of themselves as such. But while some have explained this resistance as whites' fear that their culture may be an empty void, others see this as whites' resistance to a qualified view of themselves. Much power comes at being the marker of the totality, the "mainstream."

General-interest magazines are not referred to as white magazines because targeting whites excludes an ever-growing group of people in this country and in the world—people with money to spend and who help give general-interest magazines their readership. And this raises a fascinating conflict of interest between these media and their advertisers. The editorial pages are integrated partly to expand the readership, but also because of what these images mean to whites. The ads are limited to whites because the readership is predominantly white.

Advertising representations are an important social legitimation. They sell us back ourselves, and require our participation and our reference points to do so. The trick is how best to achieve this. Traditionally, advertisers have been trained to obtain viewers' identification with models in the ads as consumers, and have assumed a one-to-one correspondence between models in the ad and users of the product. Thus, managers have been concerned that showing minorities precludes whites' identification as product users and thwarts their desire to buy.

Yet, as psychoanalytic film scholars have noted, identification is not always a precursor to desire. In fact, a whole realm of desire surfaces in the absence of identification, that is, desire for the "other." It is crucial that advertisers and media scholars get past the notion that race is a people-of-color issue. We must take a hard look at what the representation of people of color and whites means to both people of color and whites, and it is imperative that Latino and black media be included together with white media in any depiction of mainstream American media.

Creative work is only beginning to tap the rich meanings supplied by the ethnic body, and only time will tell if it will ever touch that of the ethnic mind and spirit. Images of people of color are changing from servants in white media to multiracial models in fashion layouts in white media because these images offer a fuller range of useful meanings to advertisers. The exoticism attributed to people of color has always had more to do with white culture and its refusal to acknowledge these parts of itself than to the people of color their taboos are projected upon.

The notion of *Atzlan* applied to advertising may not be quite what some had in mind. Much advertising is designed to evoke and privilege notions of affluence—which are still predominantly portrayed as white. But this is the case in white media, just as affluent images of Latinos are prevalent in Latino media and images of affluent blacks are predominant in black media. The future is here; it's just difficult to see through cultural lenses trained so long in essentialisms.

Media scholars can learn from the case of Latinos. Latino media networks have given access to us and have made the Latino market a good buy for companies by linking the various independent media scattered across the country. These media and advertisers have helped facilitate the Latino shift from various separatisms based on nationality toward a unity based on a collective Latino identity and sense of self as part of larger Latino culture. They have done so by providing a forum that paradoxically mirrors our cultural differences as Mexican Americans, Puerto Rican Americans and Cuban Americans, as well as our similarities as Latinos.

This does not mean there is no room for critiques. Advertising portrays a distorted view of Latino reality in America. In them, people are extraordinarily rich, beautiful and successful. Consumer behavior is only part of the Latino reality, and in ads it is separated from other social issues, but this is the case for all markets. As advertising scholars, we have our work cut out for us to trace these distortions and their effects on individuals, communities and society.

The ultimate affirmative action is that we Latinos have our own communities within which media and advertisements play an important role. Neither these subcultures nor their media should be viewed as a threat. Rather, Latinos' notions of the United States should be updated to consist of a cross-section of its various subcultures. This is not separatism. It is vital that each subculture retain its pride and sense of collective identity. This does not take away from Latinos' sense of themselves as Americans, and there will always be a place for those individuals and institutions that link us together.

For U.S. advertisers, *Atzlan* heralds the importance of learning to speak in the language and the images of multiple subcultures. Border people, those who tap into and resonate with more than one group, will become increasingly important. Because these "crossovers" offer economies of scale across the various specialized media, they are the future. And we will know we've arrived when we learn to see the other in ourselves.

Lisa Peñaloza is an assistant professor of advertising at the University of Illinois at Champaign-Urbana.

16

(Re)Imagining America

John Phillip Santos

Imagine this dateline: The White House, January 2044. After a brilliant career in the Senate, President Mansour Al-E Ahmad of Michigan, the nation's first Nigerian-American Muslim chief executive, has been elected to office, along with his Chicana vice president, Carmela Reyes, on the young but powerful Democratic Immigration Party ticket.

Tremendous cultural, demographic and political changes have taken place over the last 50 years to make this election possible. Perhaps most significant, NAFJA, the North American Free Jobs Agreement of 2022, dropped all restrictions to workers seeking employment in the global markets of the United States, prompting an influx of immigrants from all over the world and adding to the diversity of the nonwhite communities that now make up a majority of the U.S. population.

Just hours after his jubilant inauguration address, which began with the traditional Islamic invocation, "In the name of Allah, most benevolent, ever-merciful...," the new president takes the podium in the White House press room for his first press conference. As he looks out across the members of the White House press corps, who does he see? How many black, Latino and Asian American journalists are present? What unique cultural perspectives will they bring to bear to understand this president, and how will that affect how they report on the enterprises of his new administration?

I offer this futuristic opening scenario to illustrate a simple point: As the United States of America moves inexorably toward the fullness and complexity of its multicultural destiny, away from its historic Eurocentric origins, it is much easier to imagine the impact that shift will have on public institutions of government, state and the economy than to foresee what changes it holds for the ethics, standards and practices of the news media.

Up to now, there have been two significant initiatives aimed at achieving greater cultural diversity in American newsrooms. The first came in 1978, when the American Society of Newspaper Editors endorsed its minority employment goal of newsroom-to-society parity by the year 2000. That measure has become an unofficial professional standard helping to improve newspaper coverage of often-ignored ethnic and racial communities of the nation. Of course, although significant strides in the hiring and advancement of minority journalists have taken place, newspapers will be nowhere near achieving that goal at the millennium mark. In fact, the latest ASNE newsroom employment survey shows a slowdown in the employment of journalists of color at newspapers around the country—minorities now account for 10.49 percent of the news-editorial work force. Compare that to 1990 U.S. census figures, which show roughly 24 percent of the nation's population as nonwhite. Still, the print media deserve to be commended for raising the call. The television news industry has never espoused a similar aspiration from which its performance could be critically measured.

Demographers tell us that, even without some future "NAFJA," current population trends will produce a nonwhite majority in the United States by the middle of the next century. This will mean that to a degree unprecedented in the history of the republic, diverse cultural traditions and heritages—some refracting Western culture in unique ways, some of them *entirely* non-Western—will play an increasingly influential role in shaping the public life and the mythological imagination of the nation. The women's movement, along with ongoing struggles for gay and lesbian civil rights, is also a part of this shifting social landscape.

In this light, the model of newsroom-to-society parity and better "minority community coverage" as principal professional goals is already an anachronism. Over the next decades, as this historic transformation of American society quickens, diversity will become more and more obvious as "minorities," alone and in coalition, play ever more decisive roles in the life of the republic. We must affirm the earlier goal to achieve a fuller, more kaleidoscopic picture of our communities. But more recently, in the second significant initiative toward a more diversely informed journalism, newspapers such as the *Seattle Times,* the *Los Angeles Times,* and the *New Orleans Times-Picayune* have moved beyond the "minority news" model to recognize that sources from a multitude of ethnic and racial groups are pertinent in any general news story, and not just those concerned with, for instance, the urban minority poor.

The *Seattle Times* has even developed a checklist to help reporters become more critical regarding the extent to which their articles reflect a more diverse sampling of community points of view. That checklist ranges from a question as direct as "Have I sought a diversity of sources for this story?" to the quasi-Nietzschean self-introspection, "Am I subverting my other goals as a journalist as I seek diversity? If so, what are the alternatives?" So checklists are awkward, but they at least move such issues strongly and publicly into the worldly chatter of the newsroom.

But while hiring minority journalists, improving coverage of minority community life and increasing diversity in sourcing remain urgently needed strategies, they are not enough to guarantee a news media in touch with the dramatic internal changes the country will soon undergo. Deeper, more fundamental changes in sensibility and editorial judgment will have to take place as reporters are forced to assess the often subconscious cultural underpinnings of their journalistic practices. This will be the most difficult initiative yet because it is largely unquantifiable. For nonminority journalists, it will mean a greater commitment to recognize the cultural dimensions of stories they report. For journalists of color, it means resisting the professionally driven tendency, as one *Seattle Times* reporter termed it, "to write white," which he described as employing "a certain language, a certain code." The overarching challenge is to rid our journalism of any vestige of an "us and them" attitude, of an unspoken regard of any community or group as "others."

This is no revelation. The long-hallowed cult of journalistic "objectivity" has too often been a veneer for what is essentially a predominating white male point of view in our news culture. But in terms of journalism education and technique, what do we put in its place? Perhaps a critical subjectivity in which journalists are forced to reckon more with their own point of view in how they tell a story.

Certainly, as the nation moves, somewhat arduously, along the long arc toward an authentic and dynamic diversity of cultures, journalists must, to put it in the argot of 20th century Third World cultural struggles, "decolonize" our news media, our most important public forum of national dialogue. In short, we must reimagine journalism by engaging in the reimagining of America itself.

Over recent months, in developing a new television newsmagazine with a multicultural emphasis for public television, "Imaging America," I have had an opportunity to engage in conversations across the country about this challenge of reimagining America with a range of journalists, producers, newsroom managers, station programmers, writers, academics, performers, clergy and others from many walks of life. The intention has been to seek counsel in how to take journalistic practices and editorial judgment to a deeper multicultural sensibility. In fact, in New York City, in San Antonio, Chicago, Seattle, Miami and Los Angeles, it is a conversation that is already well under way.

In each venue, I have heard familiar complaints that the national news media fail to capture the unique regional concerns that characterize parts of the country and make of them almost nations within a nation. Some parts of the country are living a more intense encounter with multiculturalism than are others. As Sam Roberts points out in his heroic vernacularization of the 1990 census, *Who We Are: A Portrait of America,* most blacks live in eight U.S. states, most Asians in three, most Latinos in two.

There have been calls for more process-oriented coverage that will cumulatively portray the complex economic, social and political reality of, for instance, the increasingly conflicted U.S.-Mexico borderlands, the struggling far western United States, and the Southeast, which has already become a littoral of Latin America in the United States. Regarding issues of culture, the chief concern has been that the national news media, often parachuting reporters in for a story, don't appreciate the nuances that shape a community's identity in a particular city or region. In Los Angeles, one Asian American reporter speaks of the difficulties in covering an assault case in which a Korean grocer allegedly attacked a Chicano youth he suspected of having shoplifted from his store. Relations between these two groups are generally tense in L.A., so much so that when the reporter tried to interview a group of Chicano youths about the story, he was himself almost assaulted. Rather than make this a part of a story, he chose not to write about the incident at all.

Another concern many express is that the nation has very little understanding of how differentiated many minority communities are within themselves, and that monolithic references to attitudes, points of view or sentiments are a fiction: There is diversity *within* diversity, including all ideological variety, from far right to far left.

In San Antonio, one Mexican American producer stressed how little shared sensibility there is between the Chicano community that is historically rooted in the Southwest, and the Cuban expatriate communities of Florida or the urban experience of the Puerto Ricans in the Northeast. In his view, the news media tend to conflate these differences under the convenient catchall term "Hispanic."

But why are the inter-Hispanic differences important? Some have suggested such differentiations amount to a "new tribalism" that is at odds with basic American ideals. As Arthur Schlesinger asks in his recent book, *The Disuniting of America*, "The national ideal had once been *e pluribus unum*. Are we now to belittle *unum* and glorify *pluribus*? Will the center hold? or will the melting pot yield to the Tower of Babel?...What is ultimately at stake is the shape of the American future." Ironically, Schlesinger's book, filled with ambivalence about the impact of multiculturalism on America, also features as illustration Federal Express's diverse ad campaign, featuring couriers who are male and female, African American, Japanese, Caucasian. Even an Australian with a kangaroo!

The reason that differences will become increasingly important in America's polycultural future is precisely because we will be hearing voices that were never allowed to come fully forward into the arena of national attention. In fact, it is a new and more encompassing experiment in republic-building than this nation has ever attempted. Political understanding will be strained, and, more than ever, journalists will require a stronger historical knowledge of where we all come from. This will become increasingly true as national ideals of cultural and religious tolerance are being tested by Latino *Santeros* (Native Americans who use peyote ceremonially) or Muslims in cities like Dearborn, Mich., where a muezzin's public call to prayer was deemed allowable as long as its volume does not exceed that of local church bells.

At the end of 1993, *Time* addressed itself to this debate in a special issue it called "The New Face of America—How Immigrants Are Shaping the World's First Multicultural Society." The cover features a woman's face "created by a computer from a mix of several races." Though the editors clearly want to seem sympathetic to the general idea of what they dub "the first universal nation," the subtler alliances are more evident. "Even more startling, sometime during the second half of the 21st century, the descendants of white Europeans, the arbiters of the core national culture for most of its existence, are likely to slip into minority status," they write. The editors end the passage with the grim observation of one demographer: "[W]e have left the time when the nonwhite, non-Western part of our population could be expected to assimilate to the dominant majority. In the future, the white, Western majority will have to do some assimilation of its own."

In trying to foster a multicultural editorial sensibility for "Imaging America," our conversations across the country have focused on how this emerging historical prospect of retro-assimilation will affect media practices. How will that imagined future White House press corps report when the new president refers to the holy Qur'an to explicate his social and economic policies, just as presidents have always laced their dispositions with apt quotations from the Bible? How will they handle his spin doctors' (who doubts that they will still be among us?) metaphoric link between the new administration and the ancient African kingdom of Timbuktu, just as the Kennedy administration was romantically tinted by its association with the Camelot of Arthurian legend?

For now, editors, producers and journalists all must become more attentive to how cultural differences shade our shifting senses of political and social reality. One example: When the Berlin Wall came down in the fall of 1989, our print and electronic media effused with images of formerly sequestered East and West Germans showering flowers and good-will on the formerly feared border guards. The jubilation was a public affirmation of the historical triumph of justice in the collapse of a border that had long fragmented a nation.

In those very same days, the *New York Times* ran a front-page photograph from another border—the one between Mexico and the United States. In this captured image, a border guard shines his flashlight into the terrified face of a young man crawling out from beneath a tangle of steel beams. With all the brio of a hunter bagging his quarry, the caption proclaims "On the U.S.-Mexico Border a Rarity: Illegal Alien Is Caught."

Never mind that week to week, undocumented nationals are "caught" along that border by the thousands. For those of us whose Mexican heritage is in these same lands from before the time they became U.S. territory, the treatment of the image is an affront. This border, too, could fall. Nations long separated could be reunited. And a critical journalism should know how to frame and respect that sentiment, as much as it reports on the mounting waves of anti-immigrant paranoia along *la frontera*.

Indeed, the formidable task journalists face in undertaking to make journalism multicultural is how we respond to all those unexamined borders and boundaries that we have allowed to shape the way we report the life of the nation and the world around us. In most cases, it means that when we come to those borders, between cultures, between communities, between past, present and future, we do not reflexively enforce them, but rather question them and cross them.

John Phillip Santos is executive producer of "Imaging America," a new weekly newsmagazine in development at WNET-13 public television in New York City, with support from the Corporation for Public Broadcasting.

17

¡Hola, América! Newsstand 2000

Melita Marie Garza

Newspapers can see the writing on the wall, and it's in Spanish. That's why newspaper companies that once had only reporters on staff now are rushing to hire *periodistas*. That's why the companies aren't just putting out newspapers but now also publish *periódicos*. It was all inevitable in a society in which salsa now outsells ketchup.

In newspapers, as in condiments, demographics and dollars speak louder than words, no matter what the language. Between 1990 and 1993, the nation's Latino community gained more numbers than any other group, jumping from 22.4 million to 25.1 million, an increase of almost a million a year. So it's little wonder that the major media developed a mania for the Spanish-language market. It is an audience that spans the country, concentrating in states and metropolitan areas with the largest concentration of Hispanics, most notably south Florida, Texas, Chicago and Southern California.

Latino communities frequently neither seen nor heard from in the English-language major media now find themselves celebrated and covered in their own language in stand-alone publications or inserts. In south Florida, players include Knight-Ridder's well-known Spanish-language daily *El Nuevo Herald,* and the Tribune Publishing Co.'s *¡Exito!,* a weekly tabloid distributed independently of its parent paper, the Fort Lauderdale *Sun-Sentinel.* In south Texas, the *McAllen Monitor* publishes a free-standing Sunday Spanish edition, *El Monitor.* Further north, Capital Cities/ABC has weighed in with the *Fort Worth Star Telegram*'s bilingual weekly insert *La Estrella.* In Denver, Scripps Howard has come out with *Las Noticias,* a bilingual insert to the *Rocky Mountain News.* Times

129

Mirror, Gannett and the *New York Times* are also in the Spanish-language market in Los Angeles, El Paso and Santa Barbara, respectively.

Publishing companies are investing heavily to get their accent marks and tildes (~) correct. Like any other change a newspaper makes, whether it's dropping a comic strip or reformatting the TV guide, the Spanish-language effort has raised questions and concerns on all sides. All this may be Spanish, some say, but is it really news?

"We're a far cry from saying we are where we should be in terms of good hard reporting," acknowledges Mario Aranda, publisher of the Chicago version of Tribune Publishing's *¡Exito!* "*¡Exito!* is not a news daily. If our readers want 'hot coverage,' they'll have to get it from Channel 44 [Chicago's Telemundo affiliate] or the radio. We provide analysis and put things in perspective."

The newborn weekly tabloid, launched in fall 1993, focuses on culture and entertainment, usually featuring Latino celebrities and hotshots on its cover. One week the cover might feature an internationally known figure such as Chilean Cecilia Bolocco, a former Miss Universe and a current reigning queen of Spanish-language television. Less frequent are the grass-roots role models, such as Raul Raymundo, a Mexican-American who heads Chicago's Pilsen Resurrection Development Corp., a church-based nonprofit group that builds affordable homes in the Mexican-immigrant community of Pilsen.

"Until we become an institution we are using the cover as a billboard," said Aranda, who foresees *¡Exito!* maturing and evolving into harder news areas as it gains market share. "Our level of returns now is at 3.6 percent. The acceptable level [for a new publication, according to Aranda] is 15 to 20 percent," he said. But the number of copies snapped up from the newsstand haven't yet translated into profits. "Nobody makes money after seven months," Aranda said, pointing out that Fort Lauderdale's version of *¡Exito!*, which preceded the Chicago *¡Exito!* in 1991, became financially viable going into its third year.

Even some of the new Latino publications' biggest critics want to see them succeed and grow. "The development of these Spanish-language publications is a good trend," says Charles Ericksen, whose Hispanic Link News Service distributes columns in English and Spanish to both Hispanic-oriented and mainstream publications. "It's up to the community to start raising hell to make these publications of more value to the community. Right now they have little value, but they should not be discontinued," he said. "They are learning how to walk in the Hispanic community, and they are starting on the safest footing."

Some Spanish-language publications already have walked farther down the road. *Miami Herald* Publisher David Lawrence Jr., whose paper produces the daily *El Nuevo Herald,* says his publication is quite different from many of the emerging products published by the mainstream media. "First of all," he says, "it's been recognized for the past five years as the best Spanish-language paper in the country." It is also the only daily, full-service Spanish-language paper in the country. Last year, *El Nuevo*'s series on a controversial plastic surgeon, later convicted of manslaughter, won first place in the print category in the National Association of Hispanic Journalists' annual journalism awards.

"I have respect for readers and respect for people," says Lawrence, who is a past president of the American Society of Newspaper Editors. "My standards don't change because I'm dealing with a different language. To make standards different is patronizing." The *Herald,* of course, has been at the Spanish-language game a lot longer than the other major industry players, bringing out its first Latino-targeted publication 15 years ago. *El Herald,* as it was known then, also went through an evolution, revamping its format in 1987 and becoming *El Nuevo Herald.* It did not begin turning a profit until two years ago, according to Roberto Suarez, *El Nuevo*'s publisher.

The proliferation of U.S. Spanish-language papers also has sparked a debate over editorial control, with Tino Duran, president of the National Association of Hispanic Publications, leading the charge against the mainstream media for trying to "devour" minority publishers. Duran argues that the only way to preserve independent Latino voices in the newspaper industry is for mainstream papers to distribute pre-existing Latino publications rather than create their own. And some are going this route, such as the *Denver Post,* which has a distribution agreement with *El Semanario;* the *Houston Chronicle,* which distributes *La Voz de Houston;* and the *Chicago Sun-Times,* which inserts into its Sunday editions *La Raza Domingo,* a magazine produced by *La Raza,* a 25-year-old independent Spanish-language paper.

But the *Miami Herald*'s Lawrence rejects Duran's blanket condemnation of the mainstream press's efforts in Spanish-language markets, suggesting that there are many avenues to the same end. "We live in a free enterprise economy," he says. "Those who do the best job for people will have the market. Anybody working hard to reach readers I applaud."

Aranda, at Chicago's *¡Exito!,* agrees. "We are not the enemy," he argues. "The enemy is ignorance." And, he points out, "Some 70 percent of our advertisers are new to the Spanish-language market."

Further, there is also the question of how readers respond to non-English-language newspaper inserts versus freestanding publications. Some editors believe inserting Spanish-language publications into mainstream English-language papers is a culturally insensitive way to reach Latino readers. "People resent having to pay for an English-language paper just to get a few pages in Spanish," one editor said. But Lawrence, whose *El Nuevo Herald* can be obtained only in tandem with the English-language *Miami Herald,* disagrees. "We aren't hiding anything from anybody," Lawrence said. "We sell the two papers together for philosophical reasons." Lawrence believes that the two newspapers together more effectively reach a broader spectrum of the Miami-area community. "*El Nuevo* could not seek to reach everyone," he said.

Ericksen, of Hispanic Link, has a different concern over editorial control, questioning whether the content of these new mainstream Latino publications is determined by journalists or advertising sales personnel. But *¡Exito!*'s Aranda says this is precisely where his publication already is providing a superior service to the Latino community. "Most of the country's Spanish-language newspapers run on a shoestring, with little editorial staff. Editorial copy is pretty much up for sale," he argues. "That's not the case with *¡Exito!,* which carries the imprimatur of the *Chicago Tribune* and ascribes to the *Tribune*'s ethics policies."

Aranda describes how one major advertiser, who also advertises in the *Tribune,* came in seeking a favorable story in exchange for agreeing to place an ad. "I asked them if they planned to ask the same thing of the *Tribune,*" he said.

Virginia Escalante, a former journalism professor and former *Los Angeles Times* reporter, agrees that there is a difference between the economics of U.S. mainstream and Spanish-language newspapers, but not the one Aranda sees. "The trend by the major newspapers has been driven by economics—they are driven by readers as consumers," says Escalante, who is working on a doctoral dissertation at the University of California at San Diego on the history of Spanish-language newspapers. "The Latino-owned publications are driven by readers as citizens. *Nuestro Tiempo,* the Spanish-language weekly of the *Los Angeles Times,* might have its cover devoted to actor Tony Plana, while the Latino-owned publication may have the Chiapas [Mexico] uprising on its cover. The priority is determined by how they view the audience."

Despite that difference in approach, Escalante agrees that Latino-owned publications aren't necessarily any purer. "There are no saints," she observes. "The mom-and-pop Latino publications are taking liquor and cigarette ads. Their cop-out is that there is a warning posted on each ad, and they'll deny that ads for these products contribute to the ill health of the Latino community. They don't have the luxury of turning down advertisers. For example, if there is a Budweiser event in the barrio, they will probably cover it and mention in the story that Budweiser was a sponsor."

But despite the realities of economic survival, Escalante argues, "newspapers are not any old product subject to market forces. There are democratic issues implicit here. The role of the press has been that of informing citizens so they can make better decisions about policies affecting society."

Still, if a newspaper's objective is to sell information, goods or both to Latinos, some contend that using only one vehicle is the wrong approach. "If newspapers want to reach the Latino community, they need to do it in two ways," contends Rodolfo de la Garza, a professor of government at the University of Texas at Austin and vice president of the Tomas Rivera Center, a Latino think tank. "For the U.S.-born, deal with them in English. To capture the foreign-born, if they came as adults, do it in Spanish. If the industry reaches out in only one language—Spanish—newspapers will miss at least one-third to one-half of the Latino population, outside of places like Miami."

De la Garza bases his conclusions on the results of his 1989-90 study of 1,500 persons of Mexican descent. "The population [newspapers] will be excluding would be very different from the immigrant who's out there washing windows. In fact, newspapers would miss the most financially secure segment of the population, the one most likely to be buying luxury cars." De la Garza's study found immigrants acquire English rather quickly, and their children become either bilingual or English-dominant; by the third generation, they are likely to speak mostly English.

"This is a bilingual community," he observed. "There are monolingual English speakers, monolingual Spanish speakers and bilinguals, but most of the bilinguals are oral bilinguals and few of the bilinguals are sufficiently comfortable to read in the language."

As long as Latino journalists account for only 2.8 percent of all editorial employees in the nation's daily newspaper newsrooms, concerns about reaching the more assimilated Hispanic readership remain. Likewise, the lack of sensitive and informed coverage that this figure implies may ensure that Latino communities will remain invisible to the wider community.

"The thing that concerns me about Spanish-language publications is that I don't speak Spanish," says media researcher Junior Bridge, who conducts studies for the Women, Men and Media Project. "I would not like to see media companies use these publications as an excuse not to mainstream Hispanic coverage in the English-language paper."

A 1992 study she conducted of 10 leading print publications, including the *New York Times, Los Angeles Times, Chicago Tribune, Washington Post* and *USA Today,* found 4,000 news items concerning women and minorities. More than 25 percent of the articles dealt with African Americans and related issues, but only 1 percent—50 articles—dealt with Hispanics, Bridge said. The disparity is especially troubling, she points out, because black and Hispanic populations in the United States are relatively close in size. Hispanics account for about 10 percent of the U.S. population and blacks for 12 percent.

"Although the study covered July and August, a period during which two national political conventions were held to nominate presidential candidates, we gleaned no clear idea of what Hispanic voters were seeking in the candidates," Bridge said. "Most of the coverage dealt with strife, both within the Hispanic community and between the Hispanic community and other minority communities."

In his report, "Come the Millennium—Interviews on the Shape of Our Future," released by the American Society of Newspaper Editors earlier this year, David Hayes-Bautista, a noted UCLA sociologist and demographer, came to the same conclusion. "In the mainstream media, almost the only time you see a minority is in a crime or welfare story, something negative," Hayes-Bautista said. "In the Spanish-language media, you also get the human interest, the arts and sports stories you won't find in the *L.A. Times* or other papers. Latinos are reduced to only one slice in the Anglo media, while in the Spanish media, a whole community is presented.

"English-language media still reflect the gulf between the Anglo economy and what I call the emergent, predominantly minority economy," he said.

Escalante also believes the major print media "have developed two windows through which to view the society.... One of them is through the main English-language newspaper, through the dominant Anglo perspective that sees the world in a very distorted fashion. Then they have created a separate window for ethnic populations to look and talk to themselves."

Not surprisingly, one of Bridge's recommendations in her report called for the news media to diversify their staffs and news coverage. "But it won't be enough for the industry just to hire more minority reporters," she said. "It has to create a cultural environment in which that perspective can find a forum, both on the part of the person reporting that perspective as well as the people being covered."

Although mainstream media companies may be doing only half a job of reaching Latino readers, de la Garza nevertheless believes publications targeting Latino immigrants have a bright, if narrowly constructed, future. "All these newspapers primarily serve the immigrant population," de la Garza said. "As long as these immigrants keep coming, they will have readers. And I see no reason for immigration from Latin America to abate."

But if University of Chicago sociologist Douglas Massey is to be believed, the future may be even rosier for Hispanics in the United States—and so for Spanish-language publications—than de la Garza thinks. Massey believes the profoundly distinct nature of immigration under way now will change the process of assimilation itself, making Spanish all the more attractive in the long term. Unlike previous waves of immigration, the current wave is much more geographically and linguistically concentrated, with Spanish speakers accounting for almost 40 percent of all immigrants to the United States, he said.

"Large communities of Spanish speakers will emerge, lowering the economic and social costs of not speaking English and raising the benefits of speaking Spanish," Massey said. "As a result, the new immigrants from Latin America will be less likely to learn English than were their European counterparts at the turn of the century."

De la Garza argues that so far no studies support that trend. But *¡Exito!* publisher Aranda agrees with Massey that Hispanics are not following the traditional immigrant pattern. "Hispanics have more in common with occupied people than immigrants. There are elements in my being that I don't want melted away by the melting pot," said Aranda, who is Mexican-born. "One can be a good American and maintain an ability to live in two different cultures."

Contrary to de la Garza's research and other similar studies, Aranda believes that the third generation also is showing increased interest in learning and maintaining Spanish: "All the Hispanic yuppies are asking each other, 'Does your babysitter speak Spanish? Have you found a bilingual preschool yet?'"

In Miami, the *Herald*'s Lawrence sees no end in sight for Spanish-language publications. But the *Herald* also has branched outside of Spanish, running stories in some editions of the English-language *Herald* in Creole and Portuguese. "We spend millions annually on *El Nuevo Herald*," Lawrence says. "It is a very important part of what we do. I don't see the future in fewer than two languages."

Melita Marie Garza is ethnic affairs writer for the Chicago Tribune.

V
Books

18

Exploring (and Exploding) the U.S. Media Prism

Mercedes Lynn de Uriarte

Split Image: African Americans in the Mass Media
Jannette L. Dates and William Barlow.
Washington: Howard University Press, 2nd ed., 1994.

The Nature and Context of Minority Discourse
Abdul R. JanMohamed and David Lloyd, eds.
Oxford: Oxford University Press, 1990.

Racism and the Press
Teun van Dijk. London: Routledge, 1991.

Race Matters
Cornel West. Boston: Beacon Press, 1993.

Although the debate is framed in terms of participation, the real struggle over diversity in the newsroom is a conflict over points of view. Numbers alone won't change perspective. The media provide an arena for the cultural struggle that shapes images and, through them, reflects the hierarchy of social power, observe Jannette Dates and William Barlow, who explore history through the prism of hegemony in their ground-breaking book *Split Image: African Americans in the Mass Media.*

Now in its second edition, this volume traces the seldom-explored media history of dominance and resistance between blacks and whites. The book comes at a particularly relevant time when a number of indicators now point to a slowdown in the media's commitment to integration. For the third year in a row, increases in the American Society of Newspaper Editors' census of minority newsroom participation have been negligible. A 1993 report, "Muted Voices: Frustration and Fear in the Newsroom," by the National Association of Black Journalists, documents the perception gap between African-American journalists and white editors leading blacks to feel disheartened. For example, only 2 percent of managers thought that blacks were less likely to be considered for career opportunities, but 73 percent of black journalists believed that to be true. These findings support those of Ted Pease's 1991 *Newsroom Barometer* job-satisfaction study, which included the largest-ever sample of minority journalists in a random nationwide survey. It analyzed attitudes of white and minority journalists working side by side on a range of job issues, including not just career opportunities, but how white newsroom managers treated minority journalists. As a general rule, when 75 percent of white respondents said "yes" to a question concerning the role of race in the newsroom, 75 percent of minorities said "no."

Dates and Barlow remind us that the role of media is closely linked to the control of power, through which many components of dominance, including the demeaning and marginalization of "others" are expressed. Media heavily influence how people think.

Although "white owners and producers have appropriated aspects of African-American culture to enrich the mass-media mainstream and enrich themselves," they have used the power of that media to distort and marginalize black Americans, say Dates and Barlow, whose comprehensive, engagingly written research supports these claims. "The black images mass-produced by [whites], however, have been filtered through the racial misconceptions and fantasies of the dominant white culture, which has tended to deny the existence of a rich and resilient black culture of equal worth."

One strategy contributing to the power of distortion is omission, says Dutch discourse scholar Teun van Dijk. Indeed, research completed in 1989 by the National Commission on Working Women found that "Hispanics, Asians and Native Americans are virtually invisible on entertainment TV." The study indicates that blacks outnumber the total of all other minorities on prime-time TV: 65 of the 78 (83.3%) were African American, nine (11.5%) were Latino, three (4.3%) were Asian and one (1.3%) was Native American. Almost all these were middle-class or wealthy characters. This contributes to the polarity of minority representation on television. In television news, on the other hand, minorities are overwhelmingly portrayed as deviants, criminals, illegal aliens or failures. In entertainment, they are assimilated to white middle-class lifestyles in harmonious environments, and issues of injustice are reduced to matters of individual conflict. This denies the reality of oppressive social structures, concludes the report, which also points out that only a tiny number of minorities work in decision-making positions on shows with minority characters.

Eradication of racism revolves around social reconstruction and the control of representation by those denied access to media decision-making and product distribution. "This war between white and black image makers and media practitioners over the African-American image is a classic example of group/class power relations, where social class divisions have been complicated by the added dimension of race," argue Dates and Barlow. This pattern is found in all "third world" experience—one defined by socioeconomic realities rather than by geopolitical location, whether domestic or external to the United States—wherever U.S. mainstream media powers dominate communicated reality. As a major exporter of media, the United States ships abroad models of denial and distortion (as Herbert Schiller, Jeremy Tunstall, and Mort Rosenblum, among others, document). At the same time, the United States imports few foreign media products, so alternative multicultural representation is minimal.

The same analogy can be made between news treatment of the economically marginalized internal and external Third World: News reflects the interests of those in power. The media convey their agendas through their content, selections of sources and structured omission of data and events. About 80 percent of all news is about those in power, observes media sociologist Herbert Gans, who labels these individuals as the "knowns." The rest of the arena is shared among "unknowns" who are mostly deviants, animals, things and abstractions. Studies since 1980 have shown little deviation from this practice. Because power in the United States is predominantly distributed along lines of race, class and gender, news mostly reflects the interests of powerful white males.

Foreshadowing of image and information conflict in the United States can be found in the work of the Commission on the Freedom of the Press headed by Robert Hutchins, University of Chicago chancellor. Conceived and funded in 1944 by Henry Luce, founder of *Time,* the Hutchins

Commission's 11 members convened as World War II drew to a close to determine the role of "free and responsible" media in a democratic society. The Commission's conclusions required the press to be inclusive, comprehensive, interactive and representative.

Their 1947 findings, summarized in *A Free and Responsible Press,* anchored media work within American traditional ideals of service and stewardship brought to the defense of the First Amendment. "It goes without saying that the responsibilities of the owners and managers of the press are to their consciences and the common good for the formation of public opinion," the Commission observed. "The relative power of the press carries with it relatively great obligations." Those obligations, the panel said, are to the society and its citizens. In a democracy, the press provides forums through which to identify common interests and build community. It interprets citizens to one another. "People make decisions in large part in terms of favorable or unfavorable images," the commissioners said. "When images [in the media] fail to present the social group truly, they tend to pervert judgment." In the first of five standards of professionalism they said are required in a responsible press, the Commission concluded that the press must present news "in a context which gives it meaning." Representative portrayal of "constituent groups in society," the Commission noted in another standard, also is a must.

The Hutchins Commission recognized that freedom of expression belongs to the people. In relation to media, this freedom is exercised through access to the press, which generates forums for debate that contribute to a society's refinement of its ideas and values. But these white, Ivy League men acknowledged that there exists a potential that such expression would be blocked by the media. "The press is not free," they wrote, "if those who operate it behave as though their position conferred on them the privilege of being deaf to ideas which the process of free speech has brought to public attention."

Just 20 years after the Hutchins Commission published its report, President Lyndon Baines Johnson appointed the National Advisory Commission on Civil Disorders to determine the causes behind more than 150 racial disturbances that rocked the nation in 1967, ranging from riots to smaller violent confrontations. Headed by Illinois Gov. Otto Kerner, that Commission prepared the most comprehensive government report on U.S. race relations ever produced; Chapter 15 it devoted to the press. "The media report and write from the standpoint of a white man's world," the commissioners observed. Ours was "a press that repeatedly, if unconsciously, reflects the biases, the paternalism, the indifference of white America." As a result, they concluded, the press had contributed to deep racial divisions in the nation.

Echoing the Hutchins Commission, the Kerner Commission called for context and representative reporting: "By failing to portray the Negro as a matter of routine and in the context of total society, the news media have, we believe, contributed to the black-white schism in this country." The Kerner report called for wider inclusion of blacks as reporters, editors, producers—for a full integration of the media. However, it would take a number of discrimination lawsuits against most major mainstream media corporations before the need to integrate was taken seriously. In 1979, ASNE conducted its first annual newsroom census in an effort to encourage participation by those who have been historically underrepresented.

Nowhere is the struggle over history and image more critical than in the press, where minority participation is severely limited. Today, fewer than 7 percent of all newspaper journalists are African American, about 2.5 percent are Latino, 1 percent are Asian American and .03 percent are Native American.

But compared to journalism education, the industry is light years ahead. In the 1990s, fewer than 5 percent of all journalism and mass communication educators are minorities; if one counts only those that are tenured, the numbers drop significantly. Courses to teach students how to cover underrepresented communities are virtually nonexistent.

Along with scarce participation goes content distortion or omission. Minority issues are not deemed newsworthy or are only found to be so in descriptions of deviance. *Webster's* defines hegemony as "preponderant influence or authority esp. of one nation over another." In mass communication, the ideology of objectivity operates to reinforce the mechanics of hegemony—the pervasive definitions of "what is" that become the assumptions or "common sense" upon which society revolves.

Gans defined the core around which news stories are constructed as a set of six prevailing values: ethnocentrism, altruistic democracy, responsible capitalism, small-town pastoralism, individualism and moderatism. These values are defined through and define the mythologized American experience. This experience, portrayed by the press, says Gans, is perceived through a "public, business and professional, upper-middle-class, middle-aged white male" perspective.

A homogeneity that denies race, class and gender conflict and, through the use of content and sources, constructs a hegemonic reality is, in fact, an ideology. It is the construction of a belief system that supports a prevailing distribution of power. As media scholar Herbert Altschull points out in *Agents of Power,* regardless of the system in which it operates, news media serve to reinforce the status quo. Until the 1970s, in the United States that meant a system of both legislated and *de facto* segregation. The civil rights movement challenged that, but changing a history of institutionalized racism remains difficult. Indeed, the conceptual tools that permit us to recognize and understand racism are still evolving. This is true both in newsrooms and in journalism education.

At first, many people thought that numbers defined segregation, that by adding a demographic mix to the workplace and the academy, racism would be eliminated. It was perhaps a reasonable first assumption. If racism depended upon exclusion, then inclusion would remove the problem. The first lawsuits and professional censuses supported this premise: How many of what kind of Americans could be found in a given work site? Affirmative action addressed numbers. It required slicing the same pie for different distribution, but, except for defending these hiring practices on the grounds of social justice, affirmative action ignores the intellectual, economic and political aspects of power redistribution that territorial changes imply. This was especially unwise for the press, because it had never dealt at all with race relations. Media convey definitions of reality, both expressed and implicit. Upon these definitions cultural "truths" are constructed and maintained. "The mass media," says Teun van Dijk in *Racism and the Press,* "provide an ideological framework for the interpretation of ethnic events. This framework may also act as a legitimation for prejudices and discrimination against minority groups."

The power of news media is strengthened by distance. This is especially the case in matters of race where a society remains segregated, however informally. Few readers have direct knowledge of reported incidents; they must therefore justify granting the press significant credibility. The media claim "objectivity" to warrant such trust. But "objectivity" has long been white and largely remains so today. Whites perceive the world through a grid compatible to the news media's definition. It is a definition generated by a white male-dominated industry at a time when marketing news through then-emerging mass services like the Associated Press required a concept that would make the news product attractive to publishers and editors regardless of locale or political philosophy. Largely for that reason, the distorted, negative caricature of black image that Dates and Barlow (as well as others) document were rarely explored or addressed. When they were, it was only in the most superficial terms, usually on an offensive case-by-case basis. Indeed, the concept of "objectivity" prevents such exploration because it provides a circular reasoning by assuming publication as both measure and proof of fairness, a standard still defined and defended by decision-makers, from reporters to editors. Challenges to coverage are usually labeled as bias and dismissed, except in the most blatant instances. As a result, little media attention is devoted to the intellectual structure provided by social institutions like family, religion, education, or to the economic structures that distribute well-being along established lines of participation. Social control is mostly sustained around the way we think. Those perceptions will not be challenged without intellectual diversity—including in newsrooms. For the time being, in terms of newsthink, it is business as usual.

In their 1988 study, media researchers Jack L. Daniel and Anita L. Allen compared the coverage of blacks in *Time* and *Newsweek* with the agenda for blacks of the National Urban League. They found that the issues considered most critical by blacks—like alleviating poverty, improving education and maintaining civil rights gains—were not the focus of newsmagazine coverage. In fact, these media reflected White House perceptions of race and provided more coverage of "reverse discrimination." The unchanged focus of news, its continued reflection of government agenda, testifies to the media's resistance to change. Indeed, the media's ability to convey government priorities in the guise of objectivity indicates the ideological construct of that concept.

"Now that the discontent of blacks is no longer expressed in a violent way," notes Van Dijk in *Racism and the Press,* "the newspapers largely seem to have lost their interest in the racial situation. Also, according to black leaders and journalists, the media convey the impression that after the civil rights movement and the advances in the situation of black people, the racial problems in fact have been solved, whereas many problems have hardly changed since the 1960s. And despite increased hiring of black journalists, equal participation of black and other minorities in the media is still far from realized."

No more compelling example can be offered than the coverage and subsequent silence about events in South Central Los Angeles triggered by the 1992 racial disturbances—the most serious ever in U.S. history in terms of property damage and casualties. Within 24 hours of that conflict's start, the *Wall Street Journal* published comparative social index figures—in an article titled "How Blacks Have Fared"—documenting the lack of change between 1967 and 1990. This after a decade of conveying Reagan administration claims that racial inequities had disappeared.

But in many ways, the explosion in Los Angeles was used to underscore prevailing misperceptions. Within the first few days, the focus of blame became centered on unmarried mothers and their male sons, allegedly out of parental control, rather than on the underlying causes for their despair. Also overlooked were intransigent systems of inequity. The issues were recast by government representatives (and conveyed by media) as questions of personal morality.

Van Dijk reminds us that in matters of racial tension, "The reaction of the white public to elite definitions of the ethnic situation [is] largely fed by existing prejudices and stereotypes about ethnic minorities or (other) Third World peoples, beliefs which again largely developed because of earlier reports about similar or other 'ethnic events.'"

And Dates and Barlow note, "Stereotypes are especially effective in conveying ideological messages because they are so laden with ritual and myth."

The civil rights era inspired much new exploration of race relations, including media research and commentary. But since then there has been growing awareness of the complexity of change. The Kerner Commission call for media integration confronts that which has become the professional practice of the press, promoted in the name of "objectivity." The Kerner commissioners called for more black participation and wider coverage at a time when fewer than 1 percent of all U.S. journalists were African-American—almost all employed by the black press. But the commissioners naively assumed that integration alone would lead to changed reporting, as if, "by some mysterious alchemy," as scholar Carolyn Martindale writes, the act of employing a more diverse work force would result in more diverse coverage. Instead, minorities in the newsroom still find themselves confronting the bulwark of objectivity that excluded minority perception shaped by minority realities. Advocates of a socially responsible press find that a number of concepts like affirmative action, multiculturalism and diversity now rival the original idea of "integration." There is too little understanding that a balanced news product is not simply a matter of genetics; that there is a variety of minority voices. For, masked by all these terms, are the tougher issues of gender, class and race, which call into review issues of assimilation and cultural loyalty. These in turn revolve around the matter of power and its response to challenge. Exploring the tensions between such ideas provides some of the most compelling discourse of the contemporary critique, but it remains too often confined to narrow circles.

Foreseeing the need for wider debate as democratic societies moved toward future definitions, the Hutchins Commission urged the protection of ideas of all kinds from all directions. Commissioners repeatedly addressed the matter of access. They were particularly concerned about issues of diversity, recognizing that intellectual diversity was as much at risk as were those individuals who were marginalized: "As freedom of the press is always in danger, so it is always dangerous. The freedom of the press illustrates the commonplace that if we are to live progressively we must live dangerously." It is this point that is most often overlooked when affirmative action—rather than press ethics—motivates the debate. Press hegemony could be confronted by adhering to the five standards laid out by the Hutchins Commission 50 years ago and supported by 98 percent of member editors polled by ASNE.

But like all management, media decision-makers often seek to duplicate themselves. Assimilation has always been a one-way experience promoted as movement into a "better" society. In these terms, difference is perceived as genetically determined: "Think the same, look different." Thus, hiring a black or Latino or Asian American or Native American is perceived as promoting diversity, regardless of that individual's class, gender, attitudes or socialization.

But in sad fact, minorities are often hired for their ability to fit in rather than for their ability to provide new or diverse voices. For this reason, they are frequently seen as interchangeable, lumped together as minorities and expected to equally represent one another. Not only is this an ignorant assumption—especially in an era when racial minorities are still seeking ways to talk to *each another* about shared experiences—but it is a further confirmation that the hegemonic newsroom culture will enforce ideological objectivity.

Effective examination of these issues requires greater exchange between underrepresented groups, where "relations between them remain to be articulated," say Abdul R. JanMohamed and David Lloyd, editors of *The Nature and Context of Minority Discourse.* "Cultures designated as minorities have certain shared experiences by virtue of their similar antagonistic relationship to the dominant culture, which seeks to marginalize them all. Thus, bringing together these disparate voices in a common forum is not merely a polemical act; it is an attempt to prefigure practically what should already be the case: that those who, despite their marginalization, in fact constitute the majority should be able collectively to examine the nature and content of their common marginalization and to develop strategies for their re-empowerment."

For this to evolve in the press, newsrooms will have to become diverse. But the hiring process frequently serves to prevent this. Decisions are masked behind code phrases like "searching for a qualified minority" (editors interviewed by the Kerner Commission in 1967 complained, "We can't find qualified Negroes"; that beat (broadened to include other races) goes on a quarter-century later). This terminology usually indicates that the standard against which minority candidates are measured is a traditional white standard, the underlying implication too often being that working whites are clearly qualified, and that minorities who do not perceive the world in the same terms or whose work experience is less predictable are not.

This is a classic assimilation model. Exceptions allow the "exotic" when there is no perceived threat to power, but across the nation, business management and economic experts tell us that assimilation is counterproductive at best for a nation that must draw from diverse perspectives and talents to compete in a globalized world. "Assimilation is now generally regarded as a dysfunctional business strategy in this country because the resulting homogeneity may stifle the creativity and breadth of view that is essential to compete in today's market," notes Ann Morrison, director of leadership research at the Center for Creative Leadership in La Jolla, Calif. Affirmative action that does not bring about true substantive diversity simply toes the line of the current assimilation model.

As Cornel West, a leading African-American intellectual, tells us, "Quality leadership is neither the product of one great individual nor the result of odd historical accidents. Rather, it comes from deeply bred traditions and communities that shape and mold talented and gifted persons." In his book *Race Matters,* West argues, "Without a vibrant tradition of resistance passed on to new generations, there can be no nurturing of a collective and critical consciousness—only professional conscientiousness survives. Where there is no vital community to hold up precious ethical and religious ideals, there can be no coming to a moral commitment; only personal accomplishment is applauded. Without a credible sense of political struggle, there can be no shouldering of a courageous engagement—only cautious adjustment is undertaken."

This description fits that of the contemporary newsroom where "qualified" minorities almost uniformly are perceived to be those who are least disruptive to the newsroom culture, including its ideology of objectivity. Here the definition of newsworthiness serves to include or exclude in traditional ways despite new players in the field. Thus, the matter of integrated newsrooms is about far more than affirmative action. Resistance by members of underrepresented groups historically takes three basic forms: There are those who attempt to reform from within, those who challenge absence and distortion by alternative presentations, and those who confront exclusion with activism, ranging from lawsuits to graffiti. It is precisely along the margins of tension between professional ethics, democratic responsibility and the retention of power, that diversity applies an uneasy pressure.

Mercedes Lynn de Uriarte is a diversity consultant and associate professor in the College of Journalism and Mass Communication at the University of Texas at Austin.

For Further Reading

American Society of Newspaper Editors Human Resources Committee. *The Changing Face of the Newsroom*. Reston, Va.: American Society of Newspaper Editors, 1989.

———. *Achieving Equality for Minorities in Newsroom Employment: ASNE's Goal and What It Means*. Reston, Va.: American Society of Newspaper Editors, 1986.

Associated Press Managing Editors Association. *Minorities*. Miami: Associated Press Managing Editors Association, 1984.

Bell, Derrick. *Faces at the Bottom of the Well: The Permanence of Racism*. New York: Basic Books, 1992.

Black and White in Colour: Black People in British Television Since 1936. London: BFI, 1992.

Bogle, Donald. *Toms, Coons, Mulattoes, Mammies and Bucks: An Interpretive History of Blacks in American Film*. New York: Viking Press, 1973.

Branch, Taylor. *Parting the Waters: America in the King Years, 1954–1963*. New York: Simon & Schuster, 1988.

Brasch, Walter M. *Black English and the Mass Media*. Amherst, Mass.: University of Massachusetts Press, 1981.

The Commission on Freedom of the Press. *A Free and Responsible Press: A General Report on Mass Communication: Newspapers, Radio, Motion Pictures, Magazines and Books*. Chicago: University of Chicago Press, 1947.

Cose, Ellis. *The Rage of a Privileged Class*. New York: HarperCollins, 1993.

———. *The Quiet Crisis: Minority Journalists and Newsroom Opportunity*. Berkeley: Institute for Journalism Education, 1985.

Cripps, Thomas. *Black Film as Genre*. Bloomington, Ind.: Indiana University Press, 1978.

———. *Slow Fade to Black: The Negro in American Film, 1900–1942*. New York: Oxford University Press, 1977.

Dann, Marlin E. *The Black Press: 1827–1890: The Quest for National Identity*. New York: Putnam, 1971.

Dates, Jannette L., and William Barlow, eds. *Split Image: African Americans in the Mass Media*. 2nd ed. Washington: Howard University Press, 1994.

Dawkins, Wayne. *Black Journalists: The NABJ Story.* Sicklerville, N.J.: August Press, 1993.

Dunnigan, Alice Allison. *A Black Woman's Experience: From Schoolhouse to White House.* Philadelphia: Dorrance & Co., 1974.

Duster, Alfreda M., ed. *The Autobiography of Ida B. Wells.* Chicago: University of Chicago Press, 1970.

Fielder, Virginia Dodge. *Minorities and Newspapers: A Survey of Newspaper Research.* Reston, Va.: American Society of Newspaper Editors, 1986.

Fisler, Paul L., and Ralph L. Lowenstein, eds. *Race and the News Media.* New York: Praeger, 1968.

Friedman, Lester D., ed. *Unspeakable Images: Ethnicity and the American Cinema.* Urbana, Ill.: University of Illinois Press, 1991.

Ely, Melvin Patrick. *The Adventures of Amos 'n' Andy: A Social History of an American Phenomenon.* New York: Maxwell MacMillan International, 1991.

Gates, Henry Louis Jr. *Colored People.* New York: Alfred A. Knopf, 1994.

Gates, Henry Louis Jr., ed. *Race, Writing, and Difference.* Chicago: University of Chicago Press, 1986.

Gerbner, George, and N. Signorielli. *Women and Minorities in Television Drama, 1969–1978.* Philadelphia: University of Pennsylvania Press, 1979.

Gibbons, Arnold. *Race, Politics, and the Mass Media: The Jesse Jackson Campaigns.* Lanham, Md.: University Press of America, 1993.

Ginsburg, Carl. *Race and Media: The Enduring Life of the Moynihan Report.* New York: Institute for Media Analysis, 1989.

Glazer, Nathan, and Daniel Patrick Moynihan. *Beyond the Melting Pot: The Negroes, Puerto Ricans, Jews, Italians, and Irish of New York City.* Cambridge: MIT Press, 1963.

Gossett, Thomas F. *Race: The History of an Idea in America.* New York: Schocken, 1963.

Gresson, Aaron David. *The Dialectics of Betrayal: Sacrifice, Violation, and the Oppressed.* Norwood: Ablex Publishing Corporation, 1982.

Hill, George H. *Black Media in America: A Resource Guide.* Boston: G.K. Hall, 1984.

Hill, George H., and Sylvia Saverson Hill. *Blacks on Television: A Selectively Annotated Bibliography.* Metuchen, N.J.: Scarecrow Press, 1985.

Hines, Judith D. *The Next Step: Toward Diversity in the Newspaper Business.* Reston, Va.: American Newspaper Publishers Association, 1991.

Invisible People: The Depiction of Minorities in Magazine Ads and Catalogs. New York: City of New York Department of Consumer Affairs, 1991.

Iyengar, Shanto. *Is Anybody Responsible? How Television Frames Political Issues.* Chicago: University of Chicago Press, 1991.

Jackson, Anthony W., ed. *Black Families and the Medium of Television.* Ann Arbor, Mich.: Bush Program in Child Development and Social Policy, 1982.

JanMohamed, Abdul R., and David Lloyd, eds. *The Nature and Concept of Minority Discourse.* Oxford: Oxford University Press, 1990.

Jhally, Sut, and Justin Lewis. *Enlightened Racism: The Cosby Show, Audiences, and the Myth of the American Dream.* Boulder, Colo.: Westview Press, 1992.

Johnson, Abby Arthur, and Ronald Maeberry Johnson. *Propaganda and Aesthetics: The Literary Politics of Afro-American Magazines in the Twentieth Century.* Amherst, Mass.: University of Massachusetts Press, 1979.

Leab, Daniel J. *From Sambo to Superspade: The Black Experience in Motion Pictures.* Boston: Houghton Mifflin, 1975.

Lee, Spike (with Lisa Jones). *Uplift the Race: The Construction of School Daze.* New York: Simon & Schuster, 1988.

Lentz, Richard. *Symbols, the News Magazines, and Martin Luther King.* Baton Rouge, La.: Louisiana State University Press, 1990.

Lewels, Francisco J. *How the Chicano Movement Uses the Media.* New York: Praeger, 1974.

Lyle, Jack, ed. *The Black American and the Press.* Los Angeles: Ward Ritchie Press, 1968.

MacDonald, J. Fred. *Blacks and White TV: Afro-Americans in Television Since 1948.* 2nd ed. Chicago: Nelson Hall, 1983.

Marable, Manning. *African-American Studies: Critical Perspectives on the Black Experience.* Boulder, Colo.: Westview Press, 1994.

———. *Beyond Black and White: Race in America's Past, Present and Future.* New York: Lawrence Hill, 1994.

———. *The Crisis of Color and Democracy.* Monroe, Maine: Common Outrage Press, 1992.

———. *Race, Reform and Rebellion: The Second Reconstruction.* Jackson, Miss.: University Press of Mississippi, 1991.

Martindale, Carolyn, *The White Press and Black America.* Westport, Conn.: Greenwood Press, 1986.

Martindale, Carolyn, ed. *Pluralizing Journalism Education: A Multicultural Perspective.* Westport, Conn.: Greenwood Press, 1993.

McCall, Nathan. *Makes Me Wanna Holler: A Young Black Man in America.* New York: Random House, 1994.

Miller, Randall M., ed. *Ethnic Images in American Film and Television.* Philadelphia: Balch Institute, 1978.

———. *The Kaleidoscopic Lens: How Hollywood Views Ethnic Groups.* Englewood, N.J.: Jerome S. Ozer, 1980.

Murray, James. *To Find an Image: Black Films from Uncle Tom to SuperFly.* Indianapolis, Ind.: Bobbs-Merrill, 1973.

Muted Voices: Frustration and Fear in the Newsroom. Reston, Va.: The National Association of Black Journalists, 1993.

Newman, Mark. *Entrepreneurs of Profit and Pride: From Black-Appeal to Radio Soul.* New York: Praeger, 1988.

Noble, Gil. *Black Is the Color of My TV Tube.* Secaucus, N.J.: L. Stuart, 1981.

Oak, Vishnu V. *The Negro Newspaper.* Westport, Conn.: Negro University Press, 1948.

O'Connor, John. *The Hollywood Indian: Stereotypes of Native Americans in Film.* Trenton, N.J.: New Jersey State Museum, 1980.

The Report of the National Advisory Commission on Civil Disorders. Washington: U.S. Government Printing Office, 1968.

Reeves, Jimmie L., and Richard Campbell. *Cracked Coverage: Television News, the Anti-Cocaine Crusade, and the Reagan Legacy.* Durham, N.C.: Duke University Press, 1994.

Rubin, Bernard, ed. *Small Voices and Great Trumpets: Minorities and the Media.* New York: Praeger, 1980.

Said, Edward W. *Covering Islam.* New York: Pantheon Books, 1981.

Schuman, Howard. *Racial Attitudes in America: Trends and Interpretations.* Cambridge: Harvard University Press, 1985.

Schuyler, George S. *Black and Conservative.* New Rochelle: Arlington House, 1966.

Smith, Erna. *Transmitting Race: The Los Angeles Riot in Television News.* Cambridge, Mass.: The Joan Shorenstein Barone Center for Press, Politics and Public Policy, 1994.

———. *What Color Is the News? An Ethnic Content Analysis of Bay Area News Media.* San Francisco: New California Alliance, 1991.

Sniderman, Paul M. *Race and Inequality: A Study in American Values.* Chatham, N.J.: Chatham House, 1985.

"Special Issue: Diversity in the Press." *Newspaper Research Journal.* Vol. 11, No. 3, Summer 1990.

Staples, Brent. *Parallel Time: Growing Up in Black and White.* New York: Pantheon Books, 1994.

Stein, M.L. *Blacks in Communications: Journalism, Public Relations, Advertising.* New York: Julian Messner, 1972.

Still Invisible: The Depiction of Minorities in Magazine Ads One Year After the Consumer Affairs Department Study. New York: City of New York Department of Consumer Affairs, 1992.

Streitmatter, Roger. *Raising Her Voice: African-American Women Journalists Who Changed History.* Lexington, Ky.: University Press of Kentucky, 1994.

Task Force on Minorities in the Newspaper Business. *Cornerstone for Growth: How Minorities Are Vital to the Future of Newspapers.* Reston, Va.: American Newspaper Publishers Association Foundation, 1989.

van Dijk, Teun Adrianus. *Racism and the Press.* London: Routledge, 1991.

Vincent, Theodore G. *Voices of a Black Nation: Political Journalism in the Harlem Renaissance.* Trenton, N.J.: Africa World Press, 1990.

Waters, Enoch. *American Diary: A Personal History of the Black Press.* Chicago: Path Press (distributed by Chicago Review Press), 1987.

Watkins, Mel. *On the Real Side: Laughing, Lying, and Signifying—The Underground Tradition of African-American Humor that Transformed American Culture, From Slavery to Richard Pryor.* New York: Simon & Schuster, 1994.

West, Cornel. *Race Matters.* Boston: Beacon Press, 1993.

Whittemore, Katherine, and Gerald Marzorati, eds. *Voices in Black and White: Writings on Race in America from Harper's Magazine.* New York: Franklin Square Press, 1993.

Wilson, Clint C. II, and Félix Gutiérrez. *Minorities and Media: Diversity and the End of Mass Communication.* Beverly Hills, Calif.: Sage, 1985.

Woll, Allen L. *The Latin Image in American Film.* Los Angeles: Latin American Center, University of California, 1977.

Woll, Allen L., and Randall M. Miller, eds. *Ethnic and Racial Images in American Film and Television: Historical Essays and Bibliography.* New York: Garland, 1987.

Wolper, David L., with Quincey Troupe. *The Inside Story of Television's "Roots."* New York: Warner Books, 1978.

Wolseley, Roland. *The Black Press, U.S.A.* Ames, Iowa: Iowa State University Press, 1990.

Wong, Eugene Franklin. *On Visual Media Racism: Asians in American Motion Pictures.* New York: Arno Press, 1978.

Index

157

USA Today, 49

Van Dijk, Teun, 140, 144, 145, 146
Vedder, Richard, 25
Vin Mariani, 61
Voting Rights Act (1965), 11

Walker, Kenneth R., 79
Wallace, George, 56, 85
Wall Street Journal, 146
War on drugs, 63–67
Washington Post, 48
Watkins, Mel, 86
Wausau, Wisconsin, 23–24
Weiner, Deborah, 107

Weir, Tom, 49
Welfare, immigrants and, 24–25
West, Cornel, 148–49
Whites: computer technology controlled by, 97–99; media as power agent of, 140–41, 144–45; perceptions of minority "special preference" by, 12–13; stereotypical views toward African Americans by, 14–15, 30; as "victims" of cocaine, 63
Who We Are: A Portrait of America (Roberts), 124
Wong, Jeanne, 45
Wong, William, 45–52
Woods, Keith, 107, 111